THE PEACEMAKER

THE
PEACEMAKER

MYRON S. AUGSBURGER

ABINGDON PRESS
Nashville

THE PEACEMAKER

This book is printed on acid-free paper.

Library of Congress Cataloging-in-Publication Data

Augsburger, Myron S.
The peacemaker.
1. Christian ethics—Mennonite authors. 2. Jesus Christ—Person and offices.
3. Peace—Religious aspects—Mennonites. 4. Mennonites—Doctrines.
Title.

| BJ1251.A94 | 1987 | 241'.0497 | 86-26520 |

ISBN 0-687-30353-2 (alk. paper)

All Scripture quotations in this publication unless otherwise noted are from
the Holy Bible, New International Version. Copyright © 1973, 1978, 1984,
International Bible Society.

The scripture quotation noted KJV is from the King James Version of the
Bible.

The scripture quotation noted Phillips is from The New Testament in
Modern English, copyright © J. B. Phillips, 1958, 1959, 1960, 1972.

The excerpt on page 92 is from W. H. Auden, *On This Island* (New York:
Random House, 1937), p. 47.

All quotations from *The Lausanne Covenant* are copyright © 1975 by World
Wide Publications (Minneapolis, MN 55403), and are used by permission.

MANUFACTURED BY THE PARTHENON PRESS AT
NASHVILLE, TENNESSEE, UNITED STATES OF AMERICA

To Paul and Esther Kniss,
esteemed in-laws, who have been
agents of reconciliation in thirty-five years
of Christian mission in India.

Contents

A NOTE FROM THE AUTHOR

I am indebted to many persons whose writings have enriched my life as I've sought to think with them about a Christian life-style. Since I am first of all a preacher of the gospel, my writing reflects notes from various sermons, and consequently, I cannot always provide complete references for notes that I acknowledge by quotation marks as having been taken from others. This recognition is an affirmation of my indebtedness to and involvement in the community of faith.

Also, the Bible clearly states that both male and female alike are created in the image of God, and I am deeply committed to a belief in the equality of the sexes. Therefore, I have sought to avoid sexist language in writing this book; however, when referring to the deity, I have written "he" and "him," as well as "Father," "Son," and so on, in the pattern of the biblical text.

It is my prayer that God may use this work to enrich others in God's special community of the reconciled.

Foreword

S ome months ago a Ph.D. student from Princeton University sat in my office. He said he had just completed a dissertation on the role of the churches in ridding the nation of slavery. "I have concluded," he said, "that if evangelical and conservative Christians had not become convinced that slavery is a sin, we would still have slavery in this country."

Some observers believe Christians today are in a position similar to that of the early abolitionists when they cry out against the burgeoning institutions of war-making. Those who dare to challenge deeply entrenched corporate powers of evil are met with a deafening chorus of cynical appeals to self-interest. National security is at stake, they are told, or jobs and economic well-being, or the values of civilized Christian living. So thorough is the self-deception that the Bible itself is enlisted in the defense of policies that coolly contemplate the slaughter of the innocents on a massive scale and willfully risk the destruction of all life on much of planet Earth.

In this book Dr. Myron Augsburger carefully and thoroughly develops the biblical imperative for Christian peacemaking in a nuclear age. The integrity of his biblical scholarship and the persuasiveness of his ethical reflection ought to convince not only evangelical Christians but also all committed Christians to become evangelists of *shalom* in these critical days.

With the advent of the nuclear age, Albert 11

Einstein wrote, "We shall require a substantially new manner of thinking if human kind is to survive." The manner of thinking described in this book, ancient but ever new and renewing, is the manner of thinking required in our time and quite possibly "the one authentic hope for the world."

In his interesting book *The Trimtab Factor*, business leader Harold Willens describes the function of the trimtab, the small adjustable flap on airplane wings and the rudders of ships. A great oceangoing vessel traveling at high speed can be turned and set upon a new course by the action of a small trimtab attached to the rudder. Mr. Willens believes business leaders are the trimtab of America, with the power to turn the great ship of state away from its course toward disaster.

I believe it equally likely that conservative and evangelical Christians are the trimtab of America. Their number is vast, their devotion to the Scriptures unquestionable. The core values of American culture, deeply enshrined in our corporate memories, have long been kept alive in conservative churches across the land.

Unfortunately, a crusade mentality has captured the thinking of many evangelicals in our time. Right-wing TV preachers and religious think-tanks, well funded by reactionary business interests, promote a nuclear arms build-up and a militantly anti-Soviet foreign policy, seeing "the evil empire" and "atheistic communism" as the enemy of the faith. Representing themselves as the voice of conservative Christians, they fuel the ideological battles that have breathed new energy into the Cold War, poisoning the political climate and contributing to the arms race.

To date, ten of twelve major Christian bodies in America have released extensive studies calling for a decisive change in direction in national policy. The pastoral letter of the United Methodist Council of Bishops, *In Defense of Creation,* is the latest offering. The overwhelming response that it received in the press and in governmental circles leads us to believe that the nation longs for a "substantially new manner of thinking."

Myron Augsburger gives us new hope that evangelical Christians will make their witness known with a new vigor and a new winsomeness in these violent days. The biblical mandate for all followers of the Prince of Peace is clearly revealed in these paragraphs. Authentic Christian witness to the things that make for peace could provide the citizen power to stand against the powerful, corporate forces that divert precious human resources into systems of destruction at an accelerating pace.

Walter Brueggeman points out that the intent of prophecy in the Bible is to "energize around the vision of a new possibility." A prophetic people could energize this nation around the vision of God for the human family, the vision of *shalom* so well described on these pages.

C. Dale White
BISHOP
NEW YORK AREA
THE UNITED METHODIST CHURCH

FOREWORD

The Anabaptist vision has been heralded and reviewed over the years. It is a vision that compels contemplation again and again because of its radical dimensions, but above all because of its clarion call to radical discipleship to Jesus Christ the Lord.

In recent decades there has been no more visible and prominent, international herald of this call to radical discipleship than Myron Augsburger. In *The Peacemaker*, Dr. Augsburger invites us to contemplate the compelling Christ, especially in his power as the Prince of Peace—the only True Reconciler of the divisions within humanity that ever and again threaten its Shalom.

In a time during which "true spirituality" is sought and extolled, here is a concrete—both in wholistic and global terms—expression of Christian spirituality worthy of the name. Myron Augsburger clearly and helpfully articulates the yes and the no that we must proclaim and live in the name of the Risen Christ, who empowers us to be his people in the world. In fidelity to the Word of the Risen Christ, this brother in Christ identifies critical characteristics of Christ's people in a way that both informs and encourages the thoughtful Christian to seek wholeheartedly to obey Christ. Chapter by chapter the book's argument is a persuasive apologetic for the Christian life so understood and so lived.

This book, the mature fruit of the author's rich and expansive ministry, is a worthy manifesto for those who have heard the call of the Crucified One to "come follow me." By no means least important to this faithful reflection of the Gospel is its capacity to warn followers of Jesus against cheap grace, while pointing them to authentic—and costly—grace.

Surely, the grace of the Lord Jesus Christ has informed this book and will inform, and transform, the attentive reader.

Robert P. Meye
DEAN, SCHOOL OF THEOLOGY
FULLER THEOLOGICAL SEMINARY
PASADENA, CALIFORNIA

INTRODUCTION

In this modern age, in which humanity has the capacity to destroy itself within a few minutes, there is a significant quest for meaning going on in many lives. In theological circles, attention is focused on Christology, which is the study of Christ's person and attributes. With renewed attention on Jesus, the Christ, people are asking questions about the essence of the gospel, the nature of salvation, the character of the church, the mission of the Christian in the social and political realm, and the nature of the life of discipleship. A resurgence of interest in the kingdom of Christ and its continual influence on history has engendered fresh interaction within the evangelical community on the concepts of freedom, liberation, justice, and peace. There is an awakening of concern for peace on the part of many Christians around the world who are discovering the relevance of Jesus' teachings on love and nonviolence. Believers are learning that loving their enemies is the Lord's strategy for creating a new community.

Where does a primary emphasis on Christology lead the believer on matters of moral behavior, or ethics? For the Christian, deliverance from the old life and participation in the new life in Christ means moral or ethical behavior according to the example of Jesus. For many, myself included, it leads to an ethic of peace and reconciliation. The scriptural injunction, "Make every effort to live in peace with all men and to be holy; without holiness no one will see the Lord"   17

(Heb. 12:14), clearly calls Christians to pursue an ethic of peace. While the call to holiness is prominent in this text, peace and holiness are discussed together. Peace between persons is an ethical consideration, for ethics has to do with wholeness, the regenerating, or the re-creating of dimensions of life deadened by sin. An authentic peace will not involve anything less than the wholeness of the "shalom" of God. *Shalom,* the Hebrew word for peace, denotes the well-being of the total person. God's shalom is the reconciling, healing, enriching work of his grace. God has acted, and acts, first to reconcile us to himself through Christ and then to one another in Christ. Second, God's peace, God's shalom, is expressed by creating a community with others, a community with a "covenant of peace."

Trinitarian theology affirms God as humanity's Creator, Redeemer, and Sanctifier; as Father, Son, and Spirit. Throughout history, God has been at work in grace, taking the initiative to reconcile people to himself and to one another. This is especially clear from the writings of the Old Testament prophets, men such as Micah and Ezekiel, who engaged in conflict with false prophets on the issue of peace. Isaiah announced a gospel of peace to the Israelites exiled to Babylon (Isa. 32:17; 52:7; 55:12; 57:1*a*), and this prophetic word of peace is seen in direct relation to salvation.

In Christology Christ is seen as the pre-existent Word revealing the divine life through creation, Incarnation, and sanctification. The promised new age has been ushered in by Jesus, for "he himself is our peace" (Eph. 2:14). But the mission of Christ brings no easy harmony, no quick fixes to the discord in the world. However, the wholistic work of Christ enables us to understand all creation in its true intent. Through the resurrection power in Christ, believers

18

can be engaged in the shalom of God. To share in this more fully, the Christian church will need to rediscover the relational meaning of holiness—that is, belonging totally to Christ. This wholeness can be experienced in Christ's reconciliation, in a work of grace that transforms sinful people into a community of the reconciled. As we approach the twenty-first century, this reconciliation offers the one authentic hope for the world. With the increase of global population, and consequently, increased demands for the world's resources, with violence and struggles for position and power, and with conflict between different ideologies, we need a special sense of God's call and grace for reconciling love.

In 1976, I wrote a small book on the Christian life entitled *Walking in the Resurrection.* It was a brief statement of the quality of the new life in Christ, which is an experience of transforming grace. Ever since I completed that book I have wanted to write a sequel, focusing primarily on the ethical aspects of a christological faith—a faith that sees Jesus the Christ as the full disclosure of God and the full disclosure of true humanness, and that finds in his total person the norm for thought and behavior for living by the will of God. Then, in 1983, I attended the World Congress for Itinerant Evangelists, sponsored by the Billy Graham Evangelistic Association and held in Amsterdam. While at that conference, I was asked by evangelist Luis Palau if I would consider writing a book on the biblical base for an evangelical conviction about reconciliation and nonviolence. His request gave further impetus to my thoughts of writing this volume. In tackling this important subject, I am herein recognizing the interrelation of the redemptive and the ethical aspects of our experience of Christ, and I am   19 attempting to demonstrate how faith involves character as well as creed, deed as well as word, discipleship as well as doctrine.

A theology of reconciliation is for me a theology of peace. Unfortunately, many view the emphasis on peace as if it were not a Christian witness but rather a position taken by left-wing, liberal socialists. However, many of us, as deeply committed Christians, with a high view of Scripture, and with a strong biblical realism in theology, are committed to peace because that is the way we understand Jesus. To recognize Christ as Lord is to identify with him as Savior, and also to identify with Jesus' example as our model (I Pet. 2:21-22).

The ethical counterpart of reconciliation is righteousness, that is, right-relatedness. This right-relatedness, of the believer in Christ, to God and man is in effect an ethic of peace. And this dynamic of peace, as the life in grace, offers the way to establish a new community, a fellowship of the reconciled, which will be the "salt of the earth" and "the light of the world" (Matt. 5:13a, 14a).

THE ETHIC OF THE NEW ORDER

1 Jesus calls his followers to live by the standards of the new life that he gives. He is creating a new order, a kingdom in which people live by the rule of God. This community of the reconciled finds its life and its character in Christ. This order of life is christological, hence its ethic is one of reconciliation and peace. In other words, understanding ethics as a system of morality or a standard of conduct, we can say that our conduct as Christians is built on the example of Christ. He was and is the Word of God.

Within Christian circles people have a variety of ethics. Some theologians emphasize agape love, and other people emphasize gratitude to God with appropriate behavior, and others emphasize obedience to divine law. Outside of Christian thought there are ethics of self-fulfillment and utilitarianism, as well as other systems, each being interpreted and advocated as a guide to human fulfillment. Though each emphasis may reveal parts of truth, I believe the fullest understanding of Christian conduct finds the norm for the Christian ethic defined by the person and life of Jesus Christ.

An ethic of peace can be seen as the moral aspect of a theology of reconciliation. The essence of God's peace is wholeness, the well-being of persons. And this peace, or "shalom," is a work of God's grace for the wholeness of life. Jesus himself said, "Peace I leave with you; my peace I give you. I do not give to you as the world gives" (John 14:27). His peace is not a private 21 ecstasy, a self-enjoyed entity, but rather a participation in the work of God for the well-being of all. Again, Jesus said, "I have told you these things, so that in me you may have peace" (John 16:33).

To understand an ethic of peace, one must understand two things: first, what it means to be in relationship with Christ; and second, the new order that results when we are in him. To say with Thomas Chalmers that "Christianity is Christ" means that we are Christian in relation to Christ, and we relate to Jesus as our contemporary, for he is risen, and consequently he is Lord. The joyous confession that each person makes as Christ's disciple is that "Jesus is my Lord!" Similarly, "He himself is our peace. . . . For through him we both have access to the Father by one Spirit" (Eph. 2:14, 18).

Something devastating happens to our relationship with Jesus if we move away from "salvation by faith" to "salvation by belief." Salvation by faith has to do with identifying with Jesus Christ; it has to do with a covenant, that is, a binding agreement based on his promises. Salvation by belief is more an assent to propositions, an intellectual exercise that often lacks the volitional aspects of commitment. As for mere intellectual belief, James says that "even the demons believe . . . and shudder" (James 2:19). On the other hand, saving faith does not require standing in trembling fear before a consciousness of God; it involves entering into a relationship with God. Saving faith is a relationship in which the Christian can say "Abba, Father" (Rom. 8:15).

Please note that the use of the names "Christ" and "Jesus" interchangeably in this book is deliberate, since it is my belief that the risen Jesus is Christ. I 22 believe the historical Jesus is the one Incarnation of God, the one of whom John said "the Word became flesh and made his dwelling among us" (John 1:14). The Jesus confessed as "the Christ, the Son of the living God" (Matt. 16:16) is the risen Lord Jesus Christ. The believer today meets the same Christ in faith that the original twelve disciples met and walked with two thousand years ago (see I John 1:1-3).

Samuel Miller, a distinguished professor of theology at Harvard, once said that "faith does not explain reality, it meets it." The reality we are meeting is the risen Christ. Elton Trueblood of the Quaker community, and professor of philosophy at Earlham College, comments that "to be a Christian is to bet your life that Christ is right."

To know the meaning and quality of eternal life, his followers must allow the Eternal One, the Christ, to rule in their lives. This was the issue faced by the rich young ruler as he knelt before Jesus: Would he let God be God in his life? (see Mark 10:17-22). Only in yieldedness to God, a relationship spoken of by the sixteenth-century Anabaptists as *Gelassenheit,* does one enter the fellowship of the reconciled. And this is an active yieldedness, one that delights in the will of God, not a passive yieldedness that fails to interact in reconciliation.

When we as Christians yield ourselves to God, a "new order" results, one that Paul described as a "new creation." This new order is God's work in Christ to reconcile us to himself. "If anyone is in Christ, he is a new creation; the old has gone, the new has come!" (II Cor. 5:17). This new life, which centers on Jesus, includes a commitment to his wholistic ethic.

One may ask, how does this new creature behave? What does a wholistic identification with the Master involve? How do I behave—that is, live out—my beliefs? How do I move out of a private piety to a 23 more wholistic expression of discipleship? What is the role of the believing community in interpreting the tension between word and deed, faith and obedience, and redemption and ethics?

The order or ethic of the new creation is not a philosophical ethic of utilitarianism, or one of self-fulfillment or self-esteem. Rather this ethic of the new creation finds its norm in the person of Christ, its character in his love and servant role, and its power in the inner witness of his Spirit. This identification with Christ affects one's total life, for as Paul wrote, "Those God foreknew he also predestined to be conformed to the likeness of his Son" (Rom. 8:29).

Foremost in a Christ-centered ethic is the dynamic action of God's grace. God took the initiative and moved toward humanity. God moved, and continues to move, to reconcile and make peace with humankind. In Christ God acts to overcome human rebellion, to correct the problem of estrangement, and to bring persons together in his peace (John 16:33). God's grace is dynamic; in his graciousness, he involves himself with humanity in a suffering, serving relationship.

Grace seen as God's graciousness means that grace is not a substance, nor is it a mere pronouncement; grace is a matter of presence, of acceptance. Expressed supremely in Christ, God's grace continues to be mediated to the believer by the Holy Spirit. Grace does not exclude the role of our minds or of our wills; rather, it makes possible the interaction of the mind and will with God. Instead of destroying human responsibility, God's grace effectively holds each believer accountable.

A new freedom came into my own life when I recognized that grace is God's unconditioned *yes* to me in Jesus. Paul writes that "no matter how many 24   promises God has made, they are 'Yes' in Christ"

(II Cor. 1:20). This divine affirmation is seen in history and expressed in Holy Scripture. Salvation history is the record of this continuous yes spoken by God to humanity. God expressed compassion in many ways throughout history, but did so ultimately and supremely in Jesus Christ. At the cross God said yes in spite of humanity's no. "God was reconciling the world to himself in Christ, not counting men's sins against them" (II Cor. 5:19).

This yes is also seen in the marvelous story of the prodigal son (Luke 15:11-32). When the son returned home the father welcomed him in forgiving love, moving beyond the problems to the person. He cared more about the son as a person than about what he had done. The father did not ask where his son had been or what he had been doing, but declared how good it was to have him at home. In contrast, the elder brother lacked the grace to be able to say yes.

Imagine what might have happened if the prodigal son had met the elder brother first, before he saw his father. In the same way, some persons today may be hindered from coming to God because they first encounter some unforgiving person. In this respect Jesus said that a brother's unwillingness to forgive stands against God's forgiveness: "If you do not forgive men their sins, your Father will not forgive your sins" (Matt. 6:15).

As stated earlier, the Incarnation is God's supreme yes to humanity. God entered the world in the person of Jesus of Nazareth and identified with humankind. He lived and moved among the poor and the affluent, the illiterate and the scholars, the common people and the leaders of the communities. Christ's home in Capernaum was near the synagogue, in the heart of the city, accessible to the public, open to leaders 25 and laity alike (Mark 2:2-14). God, in Jesus of Nazareth, expressed the ultimate solidarity with humanity.

God's grace, his "yes" of acceptance, places all persons in the same category. God is no respecter of persons. Jesus made clear that the privileged may often be more hesitant to receive grace than the poor, but he was not excluding the privileged. Christ's twelve disciples were not of the poorest class in society. Jesus, in grace, received all persons alike, loving the poor while also accepting the support of the wealthy (Luke 8:3).

The equality of grace is uniquely shown in the Old Testament restrictions on the numbering of the people of Israel. Each person was to pay a half shekel as an atonement or ransom for his or her life. The poor were not to pay less and the wealthy were not to pay more (see Exod. 30:15). Man's need for atonement then and now places all persons on an equal footing before divine grace. The Atonement by Christ, so understood, introduces a common "at-one-ment" for all who believe; God's divine compassion moves him to at-one-ment with us. Thus, the cross of Christ becomes central to the reconciling experience of peace (Eph. 2:14). Because God's grace, as expressed in the cross of Christ, offers the privilege of a relational reconciliation with God, a system of ethics for the Christian would appear to be basically relational. Thus, salvation is our participation in righteousness, or right-relatedness; not simply with religious laws, but with God himself (Phil. 3:9). An idealistic pietism has often spoken of righteousness in a mystical way, referring to the "righteousness of Christ" as something dropped over the believer, rather than as a relationship of identification with Christ. But righteousness may also be expressed as justice-righteousness. It is a correction

26

of the problem of estrangement, a restoration of right-relatedness. "God made him who had no sin to be sin for us, so that in him we might become the righteousness of God" (II Cor. 5:21). The emphasis of this Pauline passage is on a reconciliation that brings us into a right-relatedness with God. Consequently, our experience of God's righteousness in turn makes us an extension of God's righteousness to others. This is justice in its larger meaning—a correction of the fundamental problem of sin. Remission of sins is defined by Paul in his letter to the Romans: "Because in his forbearance he had left the sins committed beforehand unpunished—he did it to demonstrate his justice . . . to be just and the one who justifies those who have faith in Jesus" (Rom. 3:25-26). The justice of the Atonement is in a change of relationship brought about by believing in Jesus.

While grace is God's yes to us, repentant faith is the believer's unqualified yes to God. Salvation, fully offered in God's grace, is made actual in relationship by one's yes to God. Christ's redemptive mission is first one of reconciliation; and second, of re-creating in the believer the *Imago Dei*, the image of God in us, to restore him or her to authentic personhood. Thus, ethics is not a "work" added on to the experience of salvation, but an essential part of the experience. As Christians our obedient behavior as disciples is our yes to God, our yes to the lordship of Christ.

Christian ethics is essentially christological because it is based on a new covenant in Christ, a covenant of grace. This covenant is a re-creation of the fellowship lost by human sinfulness; it is a re-creation of all that is truly human. The corrective aspects of faith and repentance give rise to a new life, a new order for the community of the Spirit. To approach 27 theology christologically means that Christians relate ethics to Christ in the same way they relate salvation to Christ. In other words, a person is saved in relating to Jesus and behaves in a way that reflects this relationship.

This is no simple statement. Edward Schillebeeckx, a modern European Catholic theologian, sees "two types of Christianity, based on two types of Christology. In the one case an explicit allergy to the word 'Christ' . . . ," meaning Jesus as Lord, as ruler of all, and "in the other an obvious, sometimes aggressive and un-Christian aversion to the word 'Jesus' (of Nazareth), as though our belief were not in a concrete person but in a gnostic mystery-cult."[1] My own theological stance is that Jesus of Nazareth is also Christ the Lord. The historical Jesus was and is the absolute expression of God. My personal relationship with Christ is with the risen Jesus as Christ the Lord. He is not simply a privatistic Jesus who effected my salvation, but as Christ the Lord he is "the ruler of the kings of the earth" (Rev. 1:5) and head of the church. This means, as Schillebeeckx says, that one is to "make Jesus the prescriptive, determining factor in one's life."[2] (While I do not subscribe to Schillebeeckx's view of Scripture, I find his treatment of Christology very stimulating.)

In relation to Christ, the believer is saved, and the believer also "behaves" this relation to Christ. The Christian is part of a new order, the church, which is described in Scripture as a spiritual body with Christ as the head. The description of the church as the body of Christ, understood relationally rather than mystically, is significant to a discussion of ethics. For just as one's physical body gives visibility to one's personality, so the church makes Jesus Christ visible to the world. Ethics for the Christian becomes a means of expressing the will of God as known in the person of Jesus.

28

Christian ethics (viewed christologically) finds its character in Christ, whose example expressed the will of God in what he said, what he did, and in who he was.

As head of the church, his body, it is Christ who provides the direction for the church. Christ has committed himself to being the church's director. Like the conductor of an orchestra, he knows the potential and the limitations of each of the players. He is careful not to push the players beyond their limits lest they falter, but he does stretch them so that they will grow. To expand the biblical analogy, a healthy body functions with harmony: if all of the parts are properly related, they work together, not in opposition. In recognizing the individual believer's relation to the whole, each member is to complement the other in the body of Christ (I Cor. 12:12-26).

Now with Christ as the church's director and head, although we as Christians do not negate the ethical teachings of the Old Testament, we interpret them in light of the full disclosure of God's will in Christ. Christ has made it possible to understand the fuller meanings of the law of God. Just as we can never go back in time and relive our lives before the third grade, we cannot go back to the time before the Incarnation and live as though the "light of the gospel of the glory of Christ" (II Cor. 4:4) had not shined into our lives and the world. Jesus said, "Do not think that I have come to abolish the Law or the Prophets; I have not come to abolish them but to fulfill them," that is, he came to fill them full (Matt. 5:17). And to fill full the meaning of the commandments of God involves attitudes as well as actions, motives as much as behavior. Now we can recognize that not only is it wrong to kill people, but anything that leads to killing people is wrong (Matt. 5:21-24). Again, not only is it wrong to   29 commit adultery, but anything that leads to breaking a marriage is wrong. (See Matt. 5:27-28).

Furthermore, when we view the Ten Commandments in light of the full disclosure of God's Word, we discover the positive freedom of negative commands. The words "Thou shalt not . . . " (Exod. 20:13-17 KJV) simply limit negative behavior, they do not limit positive developments. To say "Thou shalt not kill" restricts us from killing but leaves open all positive ways to build loving relationships. To say "Thou shalt not commit adultery" prohibits adultery but provides the freedom to build love in marriage and family. Or to say, "Thou shalt not steal" restricts us from theft out of fairness to others but leaves space for us to work and manage our economic lives. The will of God, when so understood, is not a limitation imposed on us but a direction offered to us, and Jesus exemplifies that direction. He said, "I have come that they may have life, and have it to the full" (John 10:10*b*).

Peter writes,

> To this you were called, because Christ suffered for you, leaving you *an example,* that you should follow in his steps. "He committed no sin, and no deceit was found in his mouth." When they hurled their insults at him, he did not retaliate; when he suffered, he made no threats. Instead, he entrusted himself to him who judges justly. (I Pet. 2:21-23, emphasis added)

A christological approach to ethics means that rather than idolizing doctrinal or philosophical systems, we begin by taking Jesus seriously. We must reject those systems of thought, even doctrinal outlines, that decrease the uniqueness and supremacy of Jesus. 30   What he said has priority in our "doing righteousness." Jesus' words judge the systems of religious-philosophical thought that have often permitted people to rationalize the implications of Christ's teachings, especially those in the Sermon on the Mount. *What he did* becomes a model of integrity, equity, justice, and love that we are to follow. We recognize in his ultimate test at the cross the way of suffering love rather than of self-defense. Jesus chose to live and to die by the way of peace. And *what he was* becomes the norm or model for self-actualization, for the honesty by which we also can open our lives to the Father, apart from whom we are but truncated beings. Jesus modeled the true meanings of faith, prayer, fellowship, peace, and love. Christian ethics centers on Jesus Christ, who dared to say, "Anyone who has seen me has seen the Father" (John 14:9).

We become disciples of Jesus Christ by saying yes to him. Freedom and responsibility are involved in this yes (but not legalism), for when we say yes we will also say no in order to be true to our yes. The Christian is free to say no but this is done within the realm of positive action.

For one to excel in athletics, or be able to compete in the Olympics, it is necessary to say no to many other things in order to be true to the disciplines of the sport in which one participates. To achieve greatness as a pianist or a violinist, one must say no to many other enjoyable uses of one's time in order to devote long hours to practicing. In the same way, there is a cost involved in the believer's covenant with Christ and his church. In saying yes to Christ, the Christian says yes to fellowship with the church, yes to the body of Christ. One must say no to many other pursuits in order to stay true to that yes. An orchestra is a good illustration of what the church should be like—a group of 31 individuals who have mastered various instruments so that as a group they can do together what no one individual could do alone—perform a symphony.

In Christian ethics one says yes to wholeness and personhood, and therefore says no to immorality. One says yes to equity and human rights, and consequently says no to prejudice, racism, and status symbols. By saying yes to agape love, one says no to violence, war, and involvement in the nuclear arms build-up. The Christian says yes to "right to life," and thus says no to abortion. This affirmation of the "right to life" also calls the believer to say no to taking in warfare the lives of the already born.

By saying yes to the worth of all people, including the poor, the disciple of Christ says no to becoming affluent at the expense of others, and no to being indifferent toward the needy. The disciple says yes to community, and no to an individualism that is selfish and exploitative; yes to peace and no to violence, whether in spirit or in deed. A disciple says yes to joy and harmony, but no to despair and self-depreciation.

A yes has integrity only if it means that one is willing to say also no in order to be true to the yes. Even so, Christian ethics is not primarily a list of issues on which the believer says no; it is first and foremost a yes to Jesus. The New Testament speaks frequently about confessing Christ. In fact, this positive theme is more prominent than references to confessing sin (see Matt. 10:32-39; Rom. 10:9-10). It is a person's confession of Christ, and identification with him, that transforms that individual's life. And in this confession the believer's yes is an expression of loyalty, for "No one can serve two masters. Either he will hate the one and love the other, or he will be devoted to the one and despise the other. You 32 cannot serve both God and Money" (Matt. 6:24).

In some unfortunate ways, the church has lost the radical discipleship that takes Jesus with absolute seriousness. On some issues her loyalty is to Christ, but on others her first loyalty is often to an economic system, what is socially acceptable, or to an extreme nationalism. As a consequence, the church has a domesticated form of Christianity that has lost sight of the true meaning of discipleship.

In the United States in particular, churchgoers are often exponents of a civil religion rather than of the kingdom of Christ. Senator Mark O. Hatfield addressed this issue on January 31, 1973, at the National Prayer Breakfast in Washington, D.C., where before President Nixon and hundreds of world religious, social, and political leaders, he said: "If we leaders appeal to the god of civil religion, our faith is in a small and exclusive deity, a loyal spiritual adviser to power and prestige, a defender only of the American nation, the object of a national folk religion devoid of moral content. But if we pray to the biblical God of justice and righteousness, we fall under God's judgment for calling upon his name but failing to obey his commands."

When we as followers of Christ say yes to him and his kingdom, we say yes to a global kingdom that is transnational, transcultural, and transracial (Acts 28:23, 31). We become part of a network of believers around the world. This yes is a positive approach to peace, to the priorities of the "kingdom of right relationships." By saying yes to Christ, we become advocates of a "third way," one that is neither rightist nor leftist but is the way of his kingdom. Our loyalty must first be to Christ, then to our brothers and sisters in faith, and then to the people in our social-political environment. In this new order "there is no Greek or Jew, circumcised or uncircumcised, barbarian,   33

Scythian, slave or free, but Christ is all, and is in all" (Col. 3:11).

There is a myth in our society that if one has a conservative theology it must follow that one holds conservative political or social views or both. But I believe firmly that when a person has a conservative theology, and believes that Jesus is actually risen and is the Lord of his kingdom, one can be quite free to choose between conservative and liberal values in the political and social realms of all lesser kingdoms.

The "third way" is not a middle-of-the-road stance. It is not a compromise in search of the lowest common denominator. It is not a misinterpretation of tolerance as though tolerance meant a lack of conviction and commitment. It has become quite fashionable today to believe that proclaiming one's own position as being right and rejecting another's position as wrong means that one is intolerant. Actually, to be truly tolerant is to give place and opportunity to persons and ideas with which one disagrees. Those who follow the "third way" respect the voluntarism of faith, but they also take seriously their responsibility to present the evidence that has called them to the faith they themselves hold. Having been an evangelist for more than thirty years, I have carried a deep conviction that authentic evangelism does not manipulate persons, or seek to coerce their minds; rather, it seeks to communicate with the same integrity expected of a good teacher in a classroom. As believers in Christ, our mission in life is to make faith in Jesus a possibility for others.

When we take Jesus seriously for determining our ethics as well as for securing our salvation, we will understand him from the perspectives of his teaching in the Sermon on the Mount, as well as from Paul's 34 words in the Epistle to the Romans. These passages form a base for christological ethics. Paul expresses the nature of the new life, writing in chapters 1 through 8 of the book of Romans of transforming grace; in chapters 9 through 11, of reconciliation in grace; in chapters 12 through 16, of the ethical expressions of the transformed life. This ethical section bears a remarkable similarity to the teachings of Jesus in the Sermon on the Mount. This is especially true of Paul's teachings on love in the last parts of chapters 12 and 13 of Romans. We should also note that Paul is not writing to the believers in ethnic Jerusalem, but to those in Rome, the center of world political power. Even so, he is not sidetracked from the centrality of the gospel of Christ.

In summary, then, what does a commitment to Jesus have to do with ethics? I believe that commitment to Jesus makes discipleship the Christian's one vocation. Our occupational choices as Christ's disciples are to be guided by this new calling. Not only does this involve being better in one's occupation by the application of Christian principles, it also involves selectivity in our choices of occupation.

There are some occupations that cannot be sanctified simply by adding "Jesus language" or piety to the role we play, for they are contrary to the nature of Jesus and violate our commitment to him. While Jesus is Lord, not every role that he tolerates in the world is to be regarded as the scene of his activity. As Paul said, "'Everything is permissible'—but not everything is beneficial.—'Everything is permissible'—but not everything is constructive" (I Cor. 10:23; cf. I Cor. 6:12).

Commitment to Jesus also raises a question of the relationship between the sacred and the secular. Believers should not separate the two, but rather should hold them in tension, in a relationship in which they challenge each other. This means, among other 35 things, that the sacred must keep the secular from governing our lives; that the sacred must confront the secular with an integrity that exposes the perversions of the secular; and that the sacred share with the secular the common arena in which we seek the sacred. In the Incarnation, "the Word became flesh" (John 1:14). That which is sacred is to be expressed in the arena of the secular. Viewed theologically, the Incarnation means that God could become human without being sinful, hence humanness and sinfulness are not synonymous. Sinfulness is the perversion of that which is truly human. Conversely, redemption is the re-creating of the truly human, a true humanness that can only be seen and realized in Jesus.

A christological ethic is based on the full will of God as revealed and known in Jesus. "For in Christ all the fullness of the Deity lives in bodily form" (Col. 2:9). "In the past God spoke to our forefathers through the prophets at many times and in various ways, but in these last days he has spoken to us by his Son . . . " (Heb. 1:1-2). Now that the full knowledge of God's will is known in Jesus, we cannot go back to a time before the Incarnation to establish ethical norms. Believers cannot operate pre-Incarnation any more than they can ever go back to their childhood once they have become adults. Christological ethics, the ethics of the new order, seeks the full meaning of Christ's kingdom, and continually asks what it means to live under the rule of Christ in the believer's particular environment.

NOTES

1. Edward Schillebeeckx, *Jesus: An Experiment in Christology* (New York: Crossroad Pub. Co., 1981), p. 30.

2. Ibid., p. 56.

A Kingdom Theology

2 Jesus made explicit the rule of God in the lives of believers. Together we pray, "Your kingdom come, your will be done on earth as it is in heaven" (Matt. 6:10). We as disciples are now participants in his new age, which is a rule of the Spirit of God. John wrote, "You have made them to be a kingdom and priests to serve our God, and they will reign on the earth" (Rev. 5:10). Jesus announced that God's rule, the reality of the kingdom, is gospel, the Good News of "the right to become children of God" (John 1:12). In God's rule, believers have true freedom, through a new order—a new relationship with God and a new community of the reconciled. The New Testament understanding of the kingdom or reign of God is grounded in the sovereignty of God, which permeates the whole of Scripture. As clearly shown in the Old Testament, the sovereignty of God provides the guidelines and the limitations for life-style. Paul wrote, "For the kingdom of God is not a matter of eating and drinking, but of righteousness, peace and joy in the Holy Spirit" (Rom. 14:17). As such a community of "shalom," of peace, we are blessed as peacemakers and are known as the children of God (Matt. 5:9).

The dawning of this new age was announced by John the Baptist (echoing the prophet's words): "Prepare the way for the Lord, make straight paths for him" (Mark 1:3). The account of the baptism of Jesus includes the

This chapter was a lecture at Fuller Theological Seminary in the Payton Lectures, February 1985.

disclosure by the heavenly Father of the uniqueness of Jesus' messianic call. "You are my Son, whom I love; with you I am well pleased" (Luke 3:22).

God came into the world in a new and tangible expression in the person of Jesus of Nazareth (John 14:9). In him the person of God and the will of God became visible. From his baptism on, while presenting the kingdom, Jesus himself moved front and center. God disclosed himself and his kingdom in him. Jesus combined the redemptive and the ethical aspects of reconciliation; as Paul writes, God acted "through him to reconcile to himself all things, whether things on earth or things in heaven, by making peace through his blood, shed on the cross . . . to present you holy in his sight" (Col. 1:20, 22*b*). Jesus not only proclaimed the word, he actually was and is the reconciling *Word*. He fulfills the words of Isaiah the prophet, "And he will be called Wonderful Counselor, Mighty God, Everlasting Father, Prince of Peace" (Isa. 9:6*b*).

The gospel that Jesus proclaimed was that the coming kingdom was now present, for it was to be ruled by the person of the Christ. The rule of God was actually personified in Jesus, who lived by the will of God and announced the rule of God. Jesus stated to the crowds that followed him that the kingdom of God was among them (Luke 17:21). People could be part of the kingdom if they would respond in repentance and faith. This announcement reveals that there is both the "already" and the "not yet" character of the kingdom.

The kingdom was not introduced as a visible political or social structure but as the new order of spiritual priorities for all of life. This new order, breaking into society, called persons to a vocation of discipleship, to a life in the uncompromised service of God. And, following his resurrection, we are told that the

38

risen Christ led his disciples in a forty-day seminar on the reality of this kingdom of God (Acts 1:3). Jesus chose not to be a zealot, nor did he collaborate with Rome, as did the Sanhedrin. Rather, he presented a third way (explained in chapter 1), one that was captured neither by the rightist nor the leftist groups. This third way was the way of the kingdom of God.

An understanding of the kingdom of God can free us from the influence of competing ideologies. For example, in America, the church could call our government to live up to the highest ethics of its own claims, rather than try to develop a "Christian party," which would later destroy the integrity and universal mission of the church. Or again, in situations such as South Africa, which is struggling with apartheid, and where, as the *Washington Post* has stated, "all sides in South Africa invoke Christianity,"[1] the church could ask what God's rule means rather than allow this moral issue to be primarily politicized. We are to participate in God's new order, to be disciples of Christ.

As we read the New Testament, the gospel of the kingdom becomes the gospel of the King. Jesus' Sermon on the Mount may be termed "the Manifesto of the King." The Good News announced by Christ becomes the Good News of Christ. In him believers are led to conjoin the *redemptive* and the *ethical* aspects of the reconciled life. In the death and resurrection of Jesus Christ, these two aspects are held inseparably together. As Paul wrote, "He was delivered over to death for our sins and was raised to life for our justification" (Rom. 4:25).

A kingdom theology, with its ethic of peace and reconciliation, will emphasize both forgiving grace and transforming grace. As Isaiah said, "The fruit of righteousness will be peace; the effect of righ- 39 teousness will be quietness and confidence forever. My people will live in peaceful dwelling places, in secure homes, in undisturbed places of rest" (Isa. 32:17-18). This ethic is expressed in the following statement, by which I summarize my understanding of the ethics of the sixteenth-century Anabaptists: If agape love were possible without the gospel, we would need no gospel; if agape love is not possible by the gospel, we have no gospel; that agape love is possible by the gospel is what Christian discipleship is all about.

We as evangelical Christians must beware of secularizing the gospel, of extracting a Christic-principle from the gospel and divorcing it from the rule of the risen Christ himself. This secularizing would render both salvation (i.e., soteriology) and ethics impotent; salvation would be reduced to self-actualization, and ethics would be developed without the whole New Testament picture of Jesus as its norm. A christological theology, a theology of the king with his kingdom, relates salvation and ethics directly to Christ. I repeat the christological axiom I gave earlier: We are saved in relating to Jesus, and we behave—live out—our relationship with him.

Our identification with Jesus provides character for the life Paul describes as "in Christ," the life "in the heavenly realms" (Eph. 2:6). A christological ethic sees Christ as the norm for life and recognizes that he fully revealed the will of God. Paul writes of the knowledge of God, "For in Christ all the fullness of the Deity lives in bodily form" (Col. 2:9). Jesus personified the one truly human person the world has seen, for he is the one Son of man, the one expression of true humanness.

From Paul, to Athanasius, to Luther, to modern theologians, redemption has been understood as 40 the union of the divine and the human in Jesus

Christ. The believer's experience of salvation is also a union of the divine and human, for each of us is both human and born of the Spirit. When Jesus baptizes with the Spirit, the believer is indwelled and sanctified by the Spirit, is made a partaker of the divine nature, and the believer can now express the fruit of the Spirit. As Bishop Alfonzo Zulu of Zululand emphasizes, "The only branch that bears fruit is the one attached to the vine." (See John 15:4.) And to keep us aware that we must keep walking in the Spirit, we should observe that fruit is only found on the new growth.

It is the presence of the Spirit of Christ that enables his disciples to live by his ethics. Apart from him, efforts at peace are only simulated action. Jesus taught us to have an authentic relation to God. The priorities of the kingdom are love for God and love for humanity. This agape love can only be learned and experienced by identifying with Jesus.

Love involves opening one's life intimately to another person. To love God is to open one's life intimately to him; to open the heart, that is, one's affections; to open the soul, that is, one's ambition; to open the mind, that is, one's attitudes; and to open one's strength, that is, one's actions. In a similar openness, believers are to love their neighbors as themselves (Mark 12:30-31). If we as Christians open our lives fully to God, we also open our lives to what God is doing in the lives of our neighbors, whether those neighbors be friends or enemies. This second commandment hallows all of our relations with others, for love does not violate, manipulate, intimidate, or compromise.

There are various implications for the new community today when people fully identify with Jesus. The universal nature of the kingdom of God is a theological basis for peace among the world's 41 peoples. God is at work among all nations alike, reconciling them to himself and in turn to one another. Christians whose first premises begin with Christ rather than with political interests will build on this basic relationship with the person of Christ and the principles of his kingdom.

One implication of identifying with Jesus and his kingdom is identifying with the justice he expressed. The Christian is called to live at peace and to work for peace (Rom. 12:17-21), and to live in love and live by love (I John 4:7-8). Paul sees the whole law fulfilled by this agape quality of love (Rom. 13:9-10). It is in this spirit of love that justice-righteousness can be extended in society.

The nature of this justice is seen at the cross, and I call your attention again to Paul's words about the Atonement: "God presented him [Jesus] as a sacrifice of atonement . . . , so as to be just and the one who justifies those who have faith in Jesus" (Rom. 3:25, 26). Justice is here described not as paying back in kind—giving someone what they deserve—but as correcting the basic problem of sin through merciful, loving engagement with that person. Wherever persons refuse this correction, they remain alienated from God and others, but this alienation is not because God is uninterested in them. God has expressed mercy, love, and peace by his justice-righteousness. The pursuit of justice by people in any society must likewise be a careful, thorough attempt to correct the social ills that cause injustice among sinful people.

God's wrath is his righteous indignation for persons who are suffering wrong. God's wrath is a result of his deep, loving concern about holding the created order accountable. Likewise, we as Christians must live 42 accountably in relation to others, and hold one another in society accountable to the holy; and we are to model the behavior we expect from others, both in attitude and in action. As Martin Luther King said in his book *Stride Toward Freedom*, love not only avoids violence of deed but "violence of spirit." Love sanctifies personal power, and thereby keeps power from becoming tyranny; and in so doing, love promotes peace.

Jesus explained that entrance into the kingdom is wrought by a change of direction from self to God. This change is a new beginning, effected by a new birth from above, and results in a new life in the Spirit. The believer becomes one of a new people (John 3:3-5). Jesus described this new people as a new community, a *koinonia* or fellowship built upon the rock of faith-confession, a community entrusted with the "keys of the kingdom" (Matt. 16:19). This community lives under the rule of God, and expresses the claims of this rule of God in love, righteousness, and peace. John tells us, "He who does what is right is righteous, just as [God] is righteous" (I John 3:7).

Disciples of Christ accept Jesus as normative for their life-styles. When the gospel of Christ is fully expressed, it calls his followers to peace, justice, and the simple life. Daniel Migliore, professor of theology at Princeton, interprets Hans Küng as saying that "what makes Christianity special is that it considers the history of Jesus to be 'ultimately decisive, definitive, archetypal' for our relationship with God, with other persons, and with society."[2] As Christ served the Father in deed and word, so believers are to serve in deed and word.

The "keys of the kingdom," which this community holds, relates the community of faith directly to the Lord of the kingdom. The "keys" enable the church to unlock the meanings of kingdom   43 membership. By responsible action, this community is to make actual the will of God "on earth as it is in heaven." In the two references to the church in the Gospels, both found in Matthew, the church is directly related to discipline, the giving and receiving of correction (Matt. 16:18; 18:17). Only as the church takes seriously the disciplines that express the "hallowing of life" can there be any extension of this hallowing influence in society; and as Peter wrote, "It is time for judgment to begin with the family of God" (I Pet. 4:17).

According to Walter Rauschenbush, author of *The Theology for the Social Gospel,* in point four of his theology of the kingdom, "The Kingdom of God is society organized according to the will of God." Nevertheless, I see the kingdom as the *People of God,* or the church, living in the will of God within society. This is the breaking-in of a new order in society, a community within the larger community. It is the church, when truly living under the cross, that expresses the kingdom of God in the world.

Previously, I affirmed that the kingdom is happening wherever Jesus is ruling. The kingdom as a "community" within the larger social community creates a dualism in the world. As disciples of Christ we are called to be in the world but not of the world. We are to be careful that we do not let the world "squeeze [us] into its own mould" (Rom. 12:1-2, Phillips). Jesus said that we are to be sown as seed in the world, bringing forth the harvest of the kingdom. Paul spoke of his ministry as one declaring the gospel of the kingdom of God (Acts 20 and 28). Paul also spoke to believers of their having been translated from the kingdom of darkness into the kingdom of God's dear Son, now (Col.1:13).

44   The people of the kingdom are a new community of the Spirit and the body of Christ.

They take orders from the head of the body, finding new life in the Spirit. Those who know the meaning of Pentecost, of new life in the Spirit, will by faith look for new creative acts of God to break loose in the varied social orders of the world. Even among peoples under tyrannical governments, God can break in upon a people by his Spirit—God is not bound. What is more, it is the Holy Spirit who sanctifies our lives by magnifying Christ in and through us, thereby expressing the essence of the kingdom: the rule of Christ.

The body of Christ is the tangible expression on earth of what God is about. Paul said that God is making his purpose known to the principalities and powers and is expressing this purpose through the church (Eph. 3:10). The church, as was said previously, makes Christ visible to the world. The church expresses the personality of Christ. It is called to make the kingdom visible in the spirit and practice of its life—the kingdom that "is not a matter of eating and drinking, but of righteousness, peace and joy in the Holy Spirit" (Rom. 14:17). This body is known to be the church, not by its organization, but by its expression of the life of Christ.[3]

There are internal and external indications that people truly constitute the church. The internal marks are conversion and discipline; conversion in that they openly confess Jesus as Lord, and discipline in Christian worship, sacrament, and "binding and loosing" one another in the will of Christ. The external marks include involvement in evangelism-mission, and relation to the powers, or secular institutions. Of evangelism, theologian Emil Brunner has said, "The church exists by mission as fire exists by burning." With respect to the powers, the church stands under the mandate of Christ rather than under the pseudo-lordship of social, economic, or political systems. 45

I believe that Paul's words in Romans 13, "The authorities that exist have been established by God," mean that God is still above the powers. We as believers are to regard God as our authority rather than idolize the powers.

As we read and study Scripture to understand the ethical implications of Christ's lordship, we must seek the Spirit's guidance. There is a hermeneutical circle, in which the interpreter's conclusions affect his continuing interpretation. We must discern which Jesus we are seeing in the Scripture: the Jesus of western liberalism, who represents the highest ideal of authentic personhood; the sweet, cozy Jesus of pietism; the Christic-principle of much modern theology; the radically violent Jesus of leftist revolutionaries; the Jesus of success of religious hucksterism; or the Son of God-Son of Man, reconciling Suffering Servant of the Gospels.

A kingdom theology is built upon this Suffering Servant, historical Jesus—upon his birth, death, and resurrection. As God's people, the church is to further enact Jesus' inaugural comments, "The Spirit of the Lord is on me, because he has anointed me to preach good news to the poor. He has sent me to proclaim freedom for the prisoners and recovery of sight for the blind, to release the oppressed, to proclaim the year of the Lord's favor" (Luke 4:18-19). It is the limited, privatistic view of Jesus that has created the disproportionate distance between conservatives and those who see Jesus as the great liberator.

In a small-group conversation at the twenty-fifth anniversary observance of *Christianity Today* magazine several years ago, Frank Gaebelein, reflecting on theological change with a group of us at dinner, said, "We have rediscovered the presence of the

46

kingdom. Twenty-five years ago the evangelical church was saying very little about discipleship, or about the kingdom of Christ in its present manifestations." There were a few evangelical voices expressing kingdom theology at that time, including persons from the Anabaptist tradition, persons such as E. Stanley Jones in the Methodist tradition, and persons in Reformed theology, such as Jacques Ellul and David Bosch, were doing the same.

In kingdom theology, as Hans Küng points out, Jesus is seen as a nonviolent Liberator.[4] In his book *The Politics of Jesus,* which is a most significant expression of Mennonite-Anabaptist theology, Professor John Howard Yoder sees Jesus as introducing the spirit of Jubilee as God's pattern for the new age.[5] Daniel Migliore of Princeton presents an important emphasis on Jesus as incarnating and clarifying liberation. This liberation is expressed in a Spirit-filled community that is inclusive, that suffers and accepts negativism, and that celebrates the liberating grace of God here and now. This community affirms with joy that God has established a beachhead in its world to reflect freedom and justice, while it prays and works to extend the same to all people.[6] Jürgen Moltmann, a modern German theologian, says, "The friendship of Jesus cannot be lived and its friendliness cannot be disseminated when friendship is limited to people who are like ourselves and when it is narrowed down to private life . . . open friendship prepares the ground for a friendly world."[7]

Jesus modeled freedom. For example, he expressed freedom from sexual inequality in his friendships with both men and women. According to Luke 8, a significant group of women accompanied him and his disciples and helped support him from their means (Luke 8:1-3). It may thus be said that Jesus   47 appreciated sexuality without needing sex. His respect for women and men as equals was picked up by Paul in the statement that in Christ "there is neither Jew nor Greek . . . male nor female" (Gal. 3:28). What is more, Jesus answered the question of the marriage relationship by referring to the original order of creation, in that God created male and female in his own image. Paul, in I Corinthians 11, shows that the total expression of the *Imago Dei* involves both masculinity and femininity. Jesus calls us to a social maturation in marriage that relates us to one unlike ourselves.

Similarly, liberation from prejudice, racism, antisemitism, and ethnic exclusiveness is to be found in the deeper levels of community in Christ. The community of the king liberates persons to be a liberating influence in society, and to discover in him an ethic of freedom. This is the freedom of God for us, and the freedom in which persons come to recognize the creative acts of God among us. Daniel Migliore says "liberation and reconciliation presuppose each other."[8]

Jesus spoke of kingdom members as "the salt of the earth" and as "the light of the world" (Matt. 5:13-14). The Christian's influence in the world enables the world to be more truly the world God intends it to be. The believer's hallowing of life will enhance the quality of this world. The hallowing influence of Christ's peace is an enriching spirit in any society.

Believers should address persons of differing positions with discernment, and always with integrity. This is well illustrated by Jesus in his high priestly prayer. Addressing God in relation to himself, Jesus said, "Father." When he addressed God in relation to the community of disciples, Jesus used the expression "holy Father." And in addressing God in relation

48   to the world Jesus used the expression "righteous

Father" (John 17:1, 11, 25). We as believers in Christ are also to be discerning and to use integrity in our relationships, addressing persons and issues with honest identification, not with superficiality.

The hallowing influence of peace is not a power struggle, or a political action, nor does it appear to be achieved by a majority vote in the social order. People are not authentically brought to truth by political manipulation or social coercion. Rather, truth makes possible the enrichment of life by constantly raising peoples' consciousness of kingdom principles. The hallowing of life begins with small things. I am reminded of the person who, when filling in a questionnaire, came to the box marked "race" and wrote in "human."

This hallowing of life will find ways to more adequately represent Christian principles in our pluralistic society without depreciating values others embrace. The Christian does not have to negate human achievements outside of the church; all he or she needs to do is to lift Jesus higher. Such hallowing will serve to orient people to justice-righteousness issues, to human rights, to the right to life, to nonviolence, to the faith to live without nuclear arms, and to ministries to the poor and to the dispossessed. It will also extend the loving word of grace to the several billion persons in the world who are outside of Christ, and in so doing it will enable believers to discover how the church can share the suffering servant role of the Christ, for the church, too, is here to partake of dying (Col. 1:24).

Finally, though kingdom theology emphasizes peace and right-relatedness now, it also emphasizes accountability and a final judgment on the basis of kingdom priorities. The new order of Christ's kingdom, announced by John the Baptist, will be consummated 49 when the Son of Man comes again in his glory. The nations will be gathered before him, and he will divide them as a shepherd divides his sheep from his goats. The Word says,

> Then the King will say to those on his right, "Come, you who are blessed by my Father; take your inheritance, the kingdom prepared for you since the creation of the world. For I was hungry and you gave me something to eat . . . . Whatever you did for one of the least of these brothers of mine, you did for me." (Matt. 25:34-40)

If I may paraphrase Christ's next words, "Then will he say to those on his left, 'Depart from me ye cursed, into everlasting fire prepared for the devil and his angels. For I was hungry and you were obese, I was thirsty and you kept filling your swimming pools, I was naked and you were discussing fall fashions, I was sick and you said, "Let him call the doctor," I was in prison and you said, "It serves him right."'"

But Jesus also said, "By this all men will know that you are my disciples, if you love one another" (John 13:35). And again, John writes, "Anyone who does not do what is right is not a child of God; nor is anyone who does not love his brother" (I John 3:10*b*). "Dear children, let us not love with words or tongue but with actions and in truth" (I John 3:18).

Recognition of the inseparability of faith and conduct will move the church from a status quo expression of religion to an authentic discipleship. But such a movement toward true discipleship will involve our being informed Christians, involved in and aware of our culture. Without the righteousness of God, it is obvious that "born again" persons will continue to

50

reflect their cultural status quo just as a new infant is conditioned by its environment. Brunner says, "The fact that we have learned to believe does not mean that we automatically become one with the will of God."[9] Even so, as we come to believe, we can walk in God's power, for it is given fully to us when we give ourselves fully to God.

NOTES

1. Allister Sparks, *The Washington Post*, 2 October 1985.
2. Daniel Migliore, *Called to Freedom* (Philadelphia: Westminster Press, 1982), p. 43.
3. See Howard Snyder's *Community of the King* (Downers Grove, Ill.: Inter-Varsity Press, 1978).
4. Hans Küng, *On Being a Christian* (New York: Doubleday and Co., 1976), pp. 189-91.
5. John Howard Yoder, *The Politics of Jesus* (Grand Rapids: Wm. B. Eerdmanns Pub. Co., 1972).
6. Migliore, *Called to Freedom*, p. 57.
7. Jürgen Moltmann, *The Church in the Power of the Spirit* (New York: Harper and Row, Publishers, 1977), p. 121.
8. Migliore, *Called to Freedom*, p. 32.
9. Emil Brunner, *The Divine Imperative* (Philadelphia: Westminster Press, 1960), p. 148.

•

CHRISTOLOGY AND BIBLICAL INTERPRETATION

3 As carefully as we may express our views on "the full inspiration of Scripture," "the Word of God written," "the infallible rule for faith and practice," we are still left with the crucial question: How do *we* interpret the Scripture? As someone has said, "What divides us is not what the Bible says, but what we bring to the Bible." We not only ask, What does the Bible say? but, What does it *say?* Everyone comes to the Scriptures with presuppositions. In the process of interpretation, we should fully understand how those presuppositions determine how we hear what we believe the Bible says. And what we believe we hear is not necessarily what the Bible says, but our own interpretation of it.

In order to understand and live by an ethic of peace, we must be clear about our pattern of biblical interpretation. Variety in the church is owing primarily to the cultural influences on our ways of thinking and interpreting. A major question for this chapter is, How does our understanding of Christology influence our interpretation? And, following the hermeneutical circle, How does our interpretation of the Bible in turn shape our Christology?

For example, many people read the Bible without appearing to take seriously the full meaning of Christ as

---

This chapter was the basis of a lecture at Fuller Theological Seminary in the Payton Lectures, February 1985.

the Prince of Peace. To say that Christ is the center of our faith and of our interpretation raises the issue of the different meanings of Christ among Christians. For many, despite his life-style and the way in which he accepted death, Jesus does not seem to have been committed to nonviolence.

As suggested earlier, to some groups Christ may be the mediator of a private salvation; to others, the close, personal Jesus of charismatic revival; to still others, the secular Jesus of radical theology. To some he may be the abstract "Christ of God"; to some, the harmless Jesus of a liberalism seen in the human potential movement. There are those who see Jesus as a new prophet of love; to the dispossessed he may appear as a political revolutionary; to others, Christ may be an apocalyptic visionary.

To still other people, he is the historical Jesus of the Gospels, the risen Lord alive today and historically known through Scripture. This is the view of Jesus Christ that I hold, and the view that underlies my theology. Those who believe as I do refuse to separate Jesus of Nazareth from the Christ of faith; we hold Jesus Christ as our one Lord and Savior. To speak of Jesus Christ as our Lord is itself a declaration of faith, an interpretation of Jesus as we understand him through the Scriptures and through the fellowship of his disciples.

A high Christology views Jesus Christ as the Son of God—yet very much man. As the Creed of Chalcedon states, he is "very God of very God and very man of very man." In him we know what God is like, and in him we know what true humanness is like. Accepting the full witness of the Scripture about Jesus, we hear Paul's words, "For God was pleased to have all his 54 fullness dwell in him" (Col. 1:19). To interpret with a christological priority, hearing Jesus say, "The Son of Man is Lord also of the Sabbath," is quite different from those who speak of Christ's lordship but whose theological system brings him into their scheme of thought only as the needed Savior but not as sovereign Lord. Even those who build their theology on creation as the original will of a sovereign God often fail to attend adequately to the christological passages on creation where Christ's lordship is shown (John 1:1-18; Col. 1:15-19; Heb. 1:1-3).

It is with this "high Christology" that I want to discuss issues of biblical interpretation and ethics. The gospel centers on Jesus, on the whole Jesus, on the spirit in which he trod the way of the cross, on the active grace of Christ in the lives of his followers, and on the fruit of the Spirit as evidence that we are as "branches abiding in the vine" (see John 15:4-5).

I must admit, however, that our reading of Christ through the lens of modern thought influences and shapes our theology. This is seen in the impact that the humanism of Erasmus had on sixteenth-century Reformers. It is evident in the writing of Immanuel Kant, who in *Religion Within the Limits of Reason Alone*, published in 1793, thought of himself as setting forth the true moral content of Christianity. In the same way, we today are affected by three significant shapers of the modern world, Nietzsche (1844–1900), Marx (1818–1883), and Freud (1856–1939). The impact these men had on philosophy, sociology, and psychology continues to shape modern thought. Or further, for several centuries we have been shaped by the Enlightenment, and in the face of these modern streams of thought, Christian ethics has often become defensive about, rather than expressive of, the new order in Christ.   55

In ethical systems a defensive stance has failed to articulate the wholeness of a christological ethic. Much of pietism, with its strong emphasis on the vision of God, still fails to deal adequately with the social dimensions of Christian ethics. Karl Barth's "actualism" did not, in my opinion, with his existentialism, do justice to the doctrine of creation and the *Imago Dei*. Bonhoeffer's emphasis on conformity to Christ was too sacramental to prevent divergence in concrete situations. Reinhold Niebuhr's interpretation of love and justice failed to reckon adequately with redemption and the community of discipleship.[1] Situation ethics fails to recognize the structure of morality and the norm of love in the person of Jesus. Liberation theology, while attempting to focus on the historical Jesus of the Gospels, is in danger of succumbing to a Marxist form of social revolution, and diminishing the reality of sinfulness in any and all structures.

I propose that we as evangelical Christians can avoid the imbalances of various schools of thought by interpreting the Bible christologically. This was the key issue in the sixteenth century between the Reformers and the Anabaptists. The free church movement of the Reformation, sometimes called "the Radical Reformation," or "the left wing" of the Reformation, was labeled "Anabaptist" because of its re-baptism of adults. Born in Zurich, Switzerland, in 1525, the movement rejected the state church pattern of both Protestant Zwingli and the Roman Catholic Church, because of the conviction that the church answers to Christ rather than to political powers. The movement was primarily christological with its emphasis on the New Testament as the full Word of God.

I agree with the interpretation of the Anabaptist stance, as expressed by Laurence Burkholder, that

56

"the uniqueness of Anabaptist ethics lies in the fact that it accepts the New Testament as the sole norm, assuming that the ethic of discipleship in the New Testament is essentially uniform and that it is a historical necessity and possibility for the Church."[2] This approach to Scripture continues to be a key issue in our day between the advocates of an evangelical practice and those who are socially oriented, between sacramentalists and advocates of relational theology, between persons committed to peace and nonviolence and those defending militarism as necessary in a fallen world, between those who enjoy the private experiences of piety and those oriented to a corporate experience.

By hearing one another we may be able to move closer to a common center. For example, a choice statement is found in the 1967 Confession of the United Presbyterian Church: "The Bible is to be interpreted in the light of its witness to God's work of reconciliation in Christ." This statement is a hermeneutical key, just as the hermeneutical perspectives of "justification by faith" and "sovereign grace" have served as hermeneutical keys. Consideration of such perspectives takes us beyond considerations of the historical, linguistic, or contextual aspects of interpretation (while still including them), to the theological.

First, we interpret the Bible with Christ as the center and norm. Christ is the full disclosure of the person and will of God (Heb. 1:1-3). The Incarnation is final, it is the Word in flesh. Jesus of Nazareth is the fulfillment of all that the prophets spoke about. Therefore, we recognize the importance of the example and the teachings of Jesus, and we also seek to interpret the Scriptures in the spirit of Jesus' interpretations.

This approach to interpretation will help us avoid   57

the tendency to select texts from anywhere in the Bible to support a particular theme or position.

An emphasis on context means one must consider both the immediate context of a given passage or book, as well as the Bible as a whole. When interpreting a passage of Scripture, it is important to remember the adage, "A text without a context is a pretext." Applying this thought to the study of Scripture means that to see a text correctly, one must read it in relation to the sweep of salvation history. As one comes to understand revelation as an unfolding, or progressive, self-disclosure by God, one recognizes the consistency of the whole of Scripture. Fully understood, there is no contradiction of meaning in the Scripture. The consistency of the Gospels with the epistles affirms this (for example, see John 13, 14; and Mark 9, 12, in relation to Phil. 2; Rom. 12; and I Cor. 13).

Second, a christological interpretation of the Bible reveals the continuity between the old and new covenants. There is a continuous movement in the Old Testament toward the New, toward the Messiah. Jesus quoted from Isaiah 61 when he read aloud in the synagogue in Nazareth. When he finished reading, he stated that the Old Testament expectations of the Messiah were fulfilled in him (Luke 4:18-19).

This continuity between the Old and New Testaments means that we must reject a "flat book" view of the Bible. The Scripture is not written all on one level. The Anabaptist writers saw the old covenant as related to the new in a pattern of "promise" to "fulfillment."

Already in the fourth century, Augustine wrestled with this issue of the continuity between the old and new covenants. Although he did not come to the same 58 conclusions the Anabaptists did more than a thousand years later, he did look at the issue seriously. He stated that to fail to see the New Testament already introduced in the Old was to do a disservice to the Old Testament; but to fail to see that the New has something more to offer than the Old is to depreciate the worth of the New Testament.

Again there is a progression of God's disclosure from the book of Judges to the book of Amos. The book of Ecclesiastes is a philosophical statement, head and shoulders above the Greek philosophy of the day, in its conclusion that everyone is personally accountable to a personal God. Yet Ecclesiastes, theologically, is still not as circumspect as Colossians. Although both the early disclosure and the later disclosure of the Christ are one consistent body of truth, each expresses different amounts of God's self-disclosure. This, then, is a progressive revelation, just as elementary education explores the same subjects as graduate studies do, yet in a simpler way.

Let us consider a few ways in which the development of a peace ethic is directly related to a biblical hermeneutic that is christological. While God met humanity at various levels of understanding in communicating divine grace, he continued to move the perception of himself forward to a full disclosure in Jesus Christ (Acts 17:30-31). Attitudes in the Old Testament regarding slavery, women, justice, sabbath violations, and war all need to be understood in this light.

God's revelation, even in its more elementary stages, always called his people to a level of ethical behavior above that of the surrounding culture. The story of Abraham and Isaac is clearer when viewed this way. Abraham came from a culture in which sacrificing the eldest child to the gods was the expected 59 practice. When God met him under these conditions and asked for the sacrifice of Isaac, Abraham obeyed, making evident both obedience and the amazing faith that God would raise the child up and fulfill his promise. God, however, prevented the sacrifice, with a revelation that the sacrifice of human life was not part of a covenant of grace, for a gracious God need not be appeased (see Gen. 22:9-18 and Heb. 11:17-19).

Also, one can better understand Yahweh's sanction of battles in this view of an unfolding revelation. In the days of tribal gods, Yahweh was a warrior. He demonstrated by the victory of Israel over other nations his supremacy as the superior deity, but Yahweh did not continue to prove himself to the nations of the world by victory in war. Rather, the prophetic role became the more significant, with prophets as spokespersons for God, both to Israel and to the nations. In the Exile, the revelation of God came through the prophetic wisdom of Daniel, through the deliverance of the three Hebrews from the furnace and Daniel from the lions, giving clear evidence that the God of Israel was God. In the New Testament, however, it is not through national Israel that the knowledge of God is shared with the world, but through God's church in its global ministry (Eph. 3:10). In his letter to the Ephesians, Paul sets forth a contrast in moving from the particular to the universal. Thus, Jesus could say, "All authority has been given to me in heaven and on earth. Therefore, while going, make disciples of all nations" (Matt. 28:18-19 author's translation).

To say that the God of the Old Testament is not a God of peace is to overlook the meaning of the unfolding revelation that culminated in Christ. That would be as inconsistent as to say that God is not a God of forgiveness because of the stoning of

Achan and his family (Josh. 7:22-26). That God has met some people in war, at their level of "fallenness," does not mean that violence is God's primary will or part of his basic character.

The careful interpreter of Scripture must distinguish between the descriptive and the prescriptive elements of the Bible. The descriptive elements provide a framework for the unique disclosure of God. But descriptions of the behavior of Abraham, Isaac, Jacob, Judah, Samuel, David, and the others are not to be regarded in total as prescriptions for Christian behavior. The deceit, polygamy, immorality, and violence that were part of their lives are all descriptions against which we look for confrontation by God.

Although the book of Job is undoubtedly God's word, it includes humanistic speeches by Job's comforters, which are then answered by God. These speeches articulate the religious and philosophical thought of the wise scholars of Job's day, but God's answer is quite different from the thrust of those speeches. People are mistaken to quote from those speeches and say that if one is in God's will one never has to suffer, or that if a person is in the will of God, he or she will always be prosperous. We must recognize that such passages are descriptive, expressing classical humanistic philosophy, and that God breaks in later in the book to confront and oppose such philosophy.

The New Testament must also be read with this view of salvation history culminating in Christ. The passages that describe Christ's miracles illustrate this. Careful reading of these passages is very important in order to understand what Jesus is saying through the miracle. His feeding of the five thousand is not to be interpreted as making him a "bread king." Further, Jesus' compassionate answer to the Roman centurion in 61 the healing of his servant (see Matt. 8:5-13) is a description of Jesus' response to the man's faith. The important point to note is that Christ even ministered in love to a member of the Roman military establishment, which was the enemy of Israel. It is hardly consistent to say from this account that since he did not denounce the centurion's military identification, Jesus was thereby endorsing a military career. Thoughtful interpretation of Scripture calls one to distinguish between the descriptive and the prescriptive passages. In our consideration of an ethic of peace, Jesus' prescriptive statements clearly relate to nonviolence, as we can see in his extensive teachings about loving our enemies (e. g., Luke 6:25-35), and his words, "Put your sword back in its place, . . . for all who draw the sword will die by the sword" (Matt. 26:52).

A christological interpretation of Scripture sees revelation in the Old and New Testaments in the scope of salvation history, which culminates in Jesus Christ. A christological interpretation also relates symbol to meaning, interpreting the letter of Scripture by the spirit of Scripture. The Holy Spirit provides a special illumination so that the believer can understand the spirit of Scripture (I John 2:27). As Paul writes, "The man without the Spirit does not accept the things that come from the Spirit of God, for they are foolishness to him, and he cannot understand them, because they are spiritually discerned" (I Cor. 2:14).

Words are symbols, vehicles of communication; therefore, it is valuable to study the languages and cultures in which the Scriptures were written. But facility in language alone is not sufficient; interpretation must catch the basic intent of a passage. Even studying the form of Greek words does not always provide an answer. For example, in I Corinthians 12:31,

Paul writes, "But eagerly desire the greater gifts." The verb form used is exactly the same in the Greek in both the indicative and the imperative modes. Thus, one cannot be certain whether Paul was describing the Corinthians as always seeking the more impressive gifts, or whether he was commanding them to seek the better gifts.

The language of the Sermon on the Mount often calls for interpreting its basic intent rather than for preoccupation with translating it to the letter. For example, to "give to everyone who asks you" (Luke 6:30) hardly means that we are not to use the best possible judgment on how to help the needy. It is a call for believers to be sure and help those in need whatever may be the cost. This is a relevant teaching to our pastoral ministry in Washington, D.C., for we seek to discern how best to relate to "street people" and to the poor of the city without alienating them by condescension.

Third, a christological interpretation of Scripture requires a careful understanding of what the scriptural teachings implied in the historical and social environment in which they were heard. For example, in Paul's day the status of women was clearly second class or less. The Pharisee would pray each day, "God, I thank Thee that I was not born a Gentile, a slave, or a woman." Again, some rabbis even said that one might as well educate a swine as educate a woman. It was to this culture that Paul announced the nature of the new community, saying, "A woman should learn in quietness and full submission" (I Tim. 2:11). This emphasis on women learning was quite revolutionary in that culture. Unfortunately, some interpreters have stressed the word *quietness* rather than the word *learn.* In so doing, they have overlooked the point   63 that, contextually, the modesty Paul called for was a safeguard for the new freedom of women to learn.

Finally, another aspect of christological interpretation is that of the role of the reconciled community. Peter's words that "no prophecy of Scripture came about by the prophet's own interpretation" (II Pet. 1:20) may not only be relevant to avoiding proof-texting by comparing scripture with scripture, but may also include the warning to avoid the danger of individualism in interpretation. What is more, the "prophetic" role, and the role of "a word of knowledge" as gifts of the Spirit (I Cor. 12 and 14) are functions of interpretation within the believing community. Passages such as I Thessalonians 5:14-22 and Hebrews 10:23-25 emphasize the role of the gathered community of disciples to discern the will of God. The community of the reconciled becomes a hermeneutical community. This is beautifully expressed in Acts 13:2: "While they were worshiping the Lord and fasting, the Holy Spirit said, 'Set apart for me Barnabas and Saul for the work to which I have called them.'" And again, at the conclusion of the Jerusalem Conference in Acts 15, the letter sent to the churches in Asia Minor includes the statement, "It seemed good to the Holy Spirit and to us" (Acts 15:28).

Jesus' emphasis on this interpretative aspect of the believing community is expressed in Matthew 16 and 18. In chapter 16, upon Peter's confession of who Jesus was, Christ affirmed that he was giving the keys of the kingdom to the church, and what the church bound on earth should be, being bound in heaven, and what the church loosed on earth should be, being loosed in heaven (Matt. 16:19, author's translation). In chapter 18 the Lord related this role to discipline within the congregation, teaching that the community of believers is responsible for holding one another accountable to the will of God. This section of scripture concludes with the same words about "binding and loosing" that which is being bound or loosed in heaven (Matt. 18:15-20). The interpreting community is to seek the will of God together and to order its life by the divine will together.

The practice of a christological ethic can only be expected of those who share reconciliation in Christ. Short of this reconciling experience, persons will adjust Christian thought to the intellectual and cultural systems that shape their lives, and to levels of reasonable human achievement.

A christological ethic is built on a christological hermeneutic, upon the way in which Scripture is interpreted. As disciples of Christ gather around the Scripture in the spirit of Christ, something unique happens. Christ is present in their midst (Matt. 18:20), and the Holy Spirit guides them into the truth (John 16:13-15). Each person must face the test of yieldedness, of being willing to lay his or her interpretation open to the prayerful searching of the community of disciples. This includes hearing the church universal, going beyond one's in-group with its cultural sameness. To speak of the authoritative Word is to ask questions in each generation and culture about how the Word is the authority for one's own life-style.

NOTES

1. See John Howard Yoder's *Reinhold Niebuhr and Pacifism* (Scottdale, Pa.: Herald Press, 1963).
2. Laurence Burkholder, "Ethics," vol. 4 of *Mennonite Encyclopedia* (Scottdale, Pa.: Mennonite Pub. House, 1955), p. 1080.
65

JOINING THE REDEMPTIVE AND THE ETHICAL ASPECTS OF RECONCILIATION

4 The ethic of the new order is an ethic of freedom, not legalism. As stated earlier, viewed christologically, ethics is the working out of transforming grace. Jesus taught that his followers bear fruit only by abiding in him (John 15:4). Again, he told his disciples, "Apart from me you can do nothing" (John 15:5). Paul urged Christians to "work out your salvation with fear and trembling, for it is God who works in you to will and to act according to his good purpose" (Phil. 2:12-13). Believers in Christ are to work out an expression of what God is working into their experience.

Many philosophical approaches to ethics have an inherent problem of legalism, for they fail to join the ethical and the redemptive aspects of reconciliation with God. But when the redemptive is given priority, with the focus on reconciliation, the ethical takes on the wholistic characteristics of grace, peace, and love.

To avoid legalism, Christians often emphasize an ethic of gratitude. This sets ethics before us as a means of showing our gratefulness for divine grace. Such an ethic of gratitude is basically an attitude, but it does not in itself provide content. Consequently, advocates of this ethic have tended to go to the law for content and often struggle with a form of legalism.

It is the understanding of reconciliation that makes ethics relational, and that holds attitude and content together in relationship with Christ. A christological ethic takes the whole Jesus seriously, interrelating his redemptive work with his ethical expectations.

We can look at various examples in Scripture and in history that show the correct focus of interrelating the redemptive and the ethical. God's deliverance of Israel from Egypt was an act of grace in which God created a people for himself. This deliverance was followed at Sinai with the giving of the law. God began by saying, "I am the Lord your God" identifying first of all with his people; he then said, "You shall have no other gods before me" (Exod. 20:2-3). In the larger context it may be said that God redeemed the people before giving them an ethic. Redemption was primary. The Exodus has come to be a symbol in Christian faith of God's saving acts, God's deliverance of people from the bondage of sin into the freedom of new life. Reconciliation comes first, then the reconciled life follows. Freedom from legalism comes when we see that God's commandments are given under the domain of grace.

To the Corinthians Paul wrote, "Do you not know that your body is a temple of the Holy Spirit, who is in you, whom you have received from God? You are not your own; you were bought at a price. Therefore honor God with your body" (I Cor. 6:19-20). And to the Romans, Paul clearly outlined salvation as by grace; it could not be obtained by rites of religion, or by works, or by deeds of the law (Rom. 4). Following this he introduced the relationship of ethics and grace. "What shall we say, then? Shall we go on sinning so that grace may increase? By no means! . . . For sin shall not be your master, because you are not under law, but under grace . . . .You have been set free from sin and have become slaves to righteousness" (Rom. 6:1-2, 14,18). This sixth chapter of Romans is a manifesto of christological ethics.

Another very significant passage is in the second chapter of Ephesians. Having so forcefully shown that salvation is experienced by grace alone, Paul then expresses how this saving grace creates a new order of life. "For we are God's workmanship, created in Christ Jesus to do good works, which God prepared in advance for us to do" (Eph. 2:10). This is followed by an explanation of the meaning of reconciliation as revealed in the atoning work of Christ. Paul joins the redemptive and the ethical, the personal and the social, in a remarkable way, by uniting them in one reconciling grace. This passage (Eph. 2:11-22) provides an alternative to the polarization in the church between evangelism and social involvement, and between the redemptive and ethical aspects of faith.

Paul bases the ethical dimension of the reconciling work of Christ on the cross. Further, he shows that the cross reconciles members of the human family with God and with one another. He describes one of the greatest social changes imaginable, the reconciliation of Jew and Gentile: "In this one body to reconcile both of them to God through the cross" (Eph. 2:16). The cross brings to an end our hostility, both toward God and toward one another. It was in the cross that God, in Christ, laid himself bare to humanity's hostility. Christ absorbed that hostility by being a personal substitute for us. God's forgiveness is just, for Jesus paid the price of forgiving: Christ carried the full divine wrath on our sin, and by so doing released us (Rom. 3:25-26; I Pet. 2:24).

In removing the hostility existing between God   69

and men, God also removed the alienation. In Christ we are united with God and with one another.

> For he himself is our peace, who has made the two one and has destroyed the barrier, the dividing wall of hostility, by abolishing in his flesh the law with its commandments and regulations. His purpose was to create in himself one new man out of the two, thus making peace, and in this one body to reconcile both of them to God through the cross, by which he put to death their hostility. He came and preached peace to you who were far away and peace to those who were near. For through him we both have access to the Father by one Spirit. (Eph. 2:14-18)

Upon this scriptural basis, let us look at some practical implications of ethics in light of Christ's redemption. First, ethics viewed christologically is never individualistic. Rather, we are always to think in terms of relationships, both to God and to one another. Reconciliation is a movement from estrangement into fellowship. Sin isolates, grace creates community. Sin insulates, grace opens us up to fellowship. Forgiveness always takes place in the framework of a relationship, allows the relationship to be established in freedom. Man's power plays with one another vanish when he stands in a new community of freedom. In this regard, Jacques Ellul has made a significant contribution to ethical understandings, especially in his book *The Ethics of Freedom*.

Sin at its most serious is an attack on humanness. In one's personal life sin is the perversion of the good, of the *Imago Dei*. In one's social life, sin is a perversion of relationships with other persons. Sin regards another person as an "it" to be used, violates another's 70 freedom to be, and to enjoy his or her God-given potential. In religious life, sinfulness even treats God as an "it" or as a servant for one's own purposes, or rejects God by deifying oneself.

Ethics relates directly to the correction of the problem of sin in attitude and in action. There is no way in which this can happen, or be experienced, apart from joining the redemptive and the ethical aspects of reconciliation. No amount of ethical advice can, on its own, change the relationship from estrangement to fellowship. Only the gospel in its wholeness can minister to the total human predicament. This is why the evangel is "Good News," not just "good views." The news is that we are invited to be God's children.

Reconciliation is a positive relationship. Viewed from the perspective of redemption, the first ethical consideration is the restoring of the broken relationship with God. This is a return to the source of being, but it is far more personal than such words denote. Reconciliation is a restoring of the unique "Abba" relationship with God for which all humans have been created (see Rom. 8:15). The basic ethical change is the re-creating of that which was lost through human rebellion. Anything less than this would mean that ethics become an outline of good behavior without the ultimate good of opening one's life to God.

It is therefore evident that evangelism and social ethics need to be joined in the Christian's thoughts and service. Jesus was the Good News, he didn't just announce it. When we serve God with a high view of humanity, we then can also serve men, regarding all alike as created in the image of God. Social ethics will then be determined in relation to redemptive grace, which involves the restoring of each person to the higher expression of the *Imago Dei*.   71

The apostle Paul's favorite phrase to express this new relationship of redeemed humanity is the often used "in Christ." This phrase is not to be interpreted mystically, but as an expression of relationship. To experience redemption is to be reconciled, to be "in Christ" rather than outside of the fellowship of his rule. And "in Christ," in the dynamic movement of God's Spirit and reign, the new order will affect all of life, including the external orders in society. The Schleitheim Confession of the Anabaptists, drafted at their first synod in February 1527, distinguished between nonviolence for those "inside of the perfection of Christ," and the use of the sword for those "outside of the perfection of Christ," that is, outside of fellowship with Christ in the full will of God. The reconciled live in the perfection of Christ, that is, in the mature understanding of God's will, and in open relationship with him.

Ethics, when guided by Christ's redemption, will make reconciliation the groundwork of social harmony, for reconciliation involves overcoming hostility. The ethical aspect of agape love calls us to move from regarding others as enemies to regarding enemies as potential friends. God treats enemies in this way, for "while we were still sinners [enemies], Christ died for us" (Rom. 5:8). Paul wrote that the reconciliation of the cross made of two nationalities one new humanity (Eph. 2:14-18). The cross creates oneness despite diversity, and unity amidst pluralism, for "both have access to the Father by one Spirit." This unity is possible because "he himself is our peace." Such peace is only possible where God is present and at work.

Ephesians 2:11-18 teaches that it is impossible for us to preach the cross in its fullness without also proclaiming God's reconciliation and peace. The extraordinary social and political implications are obvious, for the text presents the cross as reuniting two nationalities that were once at enmity.

Because these issues of peace and reconciliation have such important implications, it is worthwhile to consider them further. At the World Congress on Evangelism in Berlin, West Germany, in 1966, I and many others witnessed a testimony of this peace. An Arab pastor from the West Bank, in Palestine, met a Jewish Christian from Israel. With intense feeling the Arab said, "I saw my people killed by your people." After a moment of electrified silence, the Israeli replied, "And I saw my people killed by your people." As we watched, suddenly both men smiled and then embraced. Afterward, they exclaimed, "Isn't it wonderful to know a Savior who forgives and makes us one!"

At the South Africa Christian Leadership Assembly, held in Pretoria in 1979, I listened to white and black speakers. They represented the communities divided by apartheid. One of the strongest appeals for faith, love, and peace was made by a Bantu lecturer. He said that unless both white and black people discovered the justice and peace of Christ, the sons of blacks would soon be killing the sons of whites, and the sons of whites would be killing the sons of blacks. Those prophetic words have since been tragically fulfilled.

In a day of a nuclear arms build-up, with the portent of global suicide, the need for this practical teaching on reconciliation is most relevant. According to the Center for Defense Information, Washington, D.C., there are 50,000 nuclear warheads in the world, 26,000 in the U.S., 20,000 in the U.S.S.R., and 4,000 among the Chinese, British, and French, so quite obviously man has the power to blow the world to bits.[1]   73

I have learned from friends in the military that modern military technology is now so advanced that even a conventional war would be so devastating that none of us can imagine the total chaos that would result. The clearest voices from the Pentagon tell us that no one would win in a nuclear war; indeed, probably no one would survive.

I believe that the construction of nuclear arsenals violates the priorities of the kingdom of God, and that this is the major moral issue facing the world today. The use of nuclear weapons would defy the sanctity of life, the stewardship of resources for the well-being of humanity, and the possibility of a future for people in this world.

The seriousness of the build-up of nuclear arsenals can be illustrated by considering the Trident submarine. On August 6, 1945, at 8:16 A.M., a small, 12.5 kiloton bomb was exploded 1900 feet above Hiroshima, Japan, a city of 348,000 persons. In that tragic event, 78,000 persons were killed at once, 48,000 were sorely wounded, 60,000 buildings were flattened, and thirty minutes later, a firestorm broke out that killed more persons than were destroyed in the first few minutes after the bomb fell. Now, we must recognize that each warhead on a Trident submarine has five times this amount of power, and the Trident has 200 such warheads—thereby making possible 1,000 Hiroshimas. Today, the U.S. could explode 11,000 warheads over the U.S.S.R., and the U.S.S.R. could explode 10,000 warheads over the U.S. The devastation possible is beyond comprehension, and the prolonged effects on the planet are unthinkable.

Martin Luther King once said, "The choice is between non-violence and non-existence." Allan Walker, a Methodist evangelist from Australia,

74

has observed that nonviolence is the message for the future of the Christian church. Former president Dwight Eisenhower once remarked, "I like to think that people want peace even more than governments [do]. In fact, I think they want it so badly that one of these days government had better get out of the way and let them have it!"

"The Church and Peacemaking in the Nuclear Age," a conference held at Pasadena, California, in May 1983, was an attempt by the diverse evangelical church to begin a dialogue on working for peace. I was privileged to be able to participate in this conference, and I was impressed by the evident increase in conviction among many conservative Christians about peacemaking. The concern over nuclear armaments has helped stimulate this new conversation. This dialogue is a move in the right direction, for, whether committed to nonviolence or to a just war, we are I believe all called to nuclear pacificism in the face of the development of nuclear arms. Technology must be viewed in relation to Christ; as Paul writes, "All things were created by him and for him" (Col. 1:16)!

Peace is an evangelical concern. The Bible is a book of peace: peace with God, peace with humankind, and peace with creation. Peace is also an evangelical concern because of the global nature of the kingdom of Christ. Finally, peace is an evangelical concern because of Christ's commission to love.

This message of peace and love is relevant in another sense, because poverty continues to increase. In a world of nearly five billion persons, the world spends $750 billion annually on military equipment, while one in three persons lives in deep poverty. It is predicted that by the year 2,000 there will be more than six 75 billion persons in the world, all needing food, shelter, and education. The ethic of love calls believers in Christ to a life-style of mutual support. To counteract the violence that will increase between the "haves" and the "have-nots," the ethic of love must enable us to serve one another.

Ethics guided by redemptive love has implications for the Christian's views of war and peace and for his or her response to poverty. Viewed from the standpoint of human need, the expenditure on arms is an affront to human rights. The Pentagon projects a $1.5 trillion expenditure over the next five years. If it had been able to spend $1 million a day from the birth of Jesus to the present, the Pentagon would still not have spent half that amount! But most serious is how these funds are being spent. Recognizing that the world is now what Marshall McLuhan has called a "global village," we cannot expect peace among peoples when the millions of hungry people ask for a slice of the economic pie, and those with the lion's share refuse to take steps to achieve equity.

Long-range programs to meet human need in developing countries, programs to share our resources with the needy, and measures to correct perversions in global ecology, are Christian callings. We should place our energies and funds on the positive side of ministering to people by providing food, shelter, education, and defense of human rights. Arms for defense are a limited security even from a humanistic perspective, for they do not contribute to the positive aspects of life. From the perspective of an ethic of peace, which is the ethic of the new order, we evangelicals should recognize the significance of John Howard Yoder's words: "When the Christian whom God has disarmed lays aside carnal

76

weapons, it is not, in the last analysis, because they are too dangerous, but because they are too weak."

In light of Christ's redemption, an ethic of peace gives priority in all of life to the reconciliation God provides. Reconciliation is the extension of divine grace in the building of the new order. The new community that results from reconciliation is spoken of in the book of Ephesians as the new household of God, for he is creating of diverse groups one new family in Christ (Eph. 2:20-22).

This new order is one in which the reign of Christ has priority. As a community of the Spirit of God this fellowship has become the "dwelling in which God lives by his Spirit" (Eph. 2:22). It is God's presence that makes us holy, that is, wholly God's. Once we were sinners, estranged from God in our rebellion, but now in grace our relation to God in faith has ended our old role as sinners and made us children of God. I am using the word *sinner* not moralistically, but relationally. We are primarily sinners not because of the bad things we have done, but because we have rebelled against God. As a result of our rebellion, we do bad things. Now, walking as children of God, we are no longer "sinners," no longer in rebellion even though we continue to sin. We as believers in Christ are called in faith to live in God's righteousness.

Righteousness means right-relatedness. The biblical word carries the meaning of justice, so we can speak of justice-righteousness, a right-relatedness that exposes all contrary positions. We render to Caesar only what is Caesar's because we have first rendered to God all that is his. Paul says that Christ "disarmed the powers and authorities" and exposed their rebellion and perversion (Col. 2:15). Seeing their true character, we will not give to the powers and authorities the loyalty 77 that belongs only to Christ. We affirm that as the risen Christ, he is Lord of the world; it is actually Christ's world, even though the principalities continue to rebel. But in this world, Christ calls his disciples to a membership in God's kingdom, where they are to live by God's rule and "seek first his kingdom and his righteousness," that is, justice-righteousness (Matt. 6:33). This call to kingdom priorities is not altered or superseded by ethnic customs, material pursuits, national patriotism, or social systems. As disciples of Christ we belong to God's commonwealth (Phil. 3:20).

In conclusion, to join the redemptive and the ethical aspects of the new life in Christ means that we as Christians have an ethical responsibility to live out the calling of God. We demonstrate our reconciliation to him by taking our place among the community of the redeemed. As John Wesley said, "God knows nothing of a solitary religion." We experience and model an ethic of community, the rightness of interpersonal responsibility. Our decision to do so moves us beyond individualism and selfishness, and helps us to participate creatively with the family of God.

A life based on the ethic of the new order models peace. This ethic is a new covenant, and it involves a commitment that will draw us beyond ourselves to participate in the divine reality of which we are witnesses. God said, "I have redeemed you . . . you are mine" (Isa. 43:1b). The christological approach to ethics takes seriously this redemption through the cross. We are redeemed, we are God's. To serve him, then, is the logical expression of our faith in him. As Paul wrote to the Romans, "Therefore, I urge you, brothers, in view of God's mercy, to offer your bodies as living sacrifices, holy and pleasing to God—this is your spiritual act of worship" (Rom. 12:1). Joining the

78

redemptive and the ethical calls us as believers to serve the highest reality—the person and will of God.

NOTES

1. The Center for Defense Information is a non-profit, non-governmental organization. How accurate these or any estimates are or can be matters less than the fact that the U.S. and the U.S.S.R. share the ability to annihilate life on earth.

DISCIPLESHIP AS LIFE-STYLE

5 In discipleship, an ethic of peace must deal honestly with the relationship between faith and works. The biblical reference to "the obedience that comes from faith" (Rom. 1:5) offers a way to resolve this tension. In some languages of the world, says global missiologist Eugene Nida, "When you think 'faith' you must think 'obedience,' and when you think 'obedience' you must think 'faith.'" In an ethic of peace, the standard is not what one says one believes, but rather what one actually does. We engage in reconciling love when we pass on to others the love that has reconciled us. Jesus said, "Not everyone who says to me, 'Lord, Lord,' will enter the kingdom of heaven, but only he who does the will of my Father who is in heaven" (Matt. 7:21).

Jesus also said, "Out of the overflow of the heart the mouth speaks" (Matt. 12:34). Goodness, in the radical sense, does not mean doing good deeds but being good persons who share themselves in love as an essential part of the deed. And "being" is a matter of inner qualities: faith, integrity, humility. It is the attitude of faith that results in the acts of love. Dietrich Bonhoeffer, in *The Cost of Discipleship* (p. 56), shows us that "only the one who believes truly obeys, and only the one who obeys truly believes."

To examine this interrelation of faith and conduct, one must first look at the interrelation of law and gospel.

This chapter was the basis of a lecture at Fuller Theological Seminary in the Payton Lectures, February 1985.

Luther once called the Old Testament law the "dialectic of the Gospel." Faith tells us that the law is not an end, but it is the expression of God, and only then of God's will. If the command to love is interpreted as law, it moves our attention from the One who commands to the thing to be done. Emil Brunner, German theologian of repute, reminds us that "it is not God's command which is to be understood as the Divine Command."[1] This is to say that the disciple in faith obeys in relation to God and not in relation to the command or the law. In the sixteenth century, Michael Sattler, the Anabaptist reformer, wrote of two kinds of obedience. Servile obedience, he said, is a legalism bound to the law, and filial obedience is an act of love, such as a son's obedience to his "father."[2]

Just as the law and the gospel correlate through our relationship with God, so it is our identifying with Christ through faith that determines obedience. My friend Donald Jacobs, a missionary for twenty years in East Africa, tells of a funeral held on the side of a Kikuyu hill. A Kenyan brother had died of wounds inflicted when he refused to take the tribal blood-oath. The reason the man had refused indicated how he viewed obedience as related to faith. He had told the tribal leaders that he had already drunk of the blood of God's lamb, and any other blood-oath would not mix with that!

When conduct expresses belief, faith is authenticated. This is the emphasis in the epistle of James in its discussion of faith and works (James 2). To better understand his meaning we might substitute the word *obedience* for *works*. His statement so translated would be significant, reading as follows:

82   You foolish man, do you want evidence that faith without deeds [obedience] is useless? Was not

our ancestor Abraham considered righteous for what he did [obedience] when he offered his son Isaac on the altar? You see that his faith and his actions [obedience] were working together, and his faith was made complete by what he did [obedience]. And the scripture was fulfilled that says, "Abraham believed God, and it was credited to him as righteousness," and he was called God's friend. (James 2:20-23)

We should note the inseparability of faith and conduct in the penultimate clause. James does not say that Abraham's obedience was imputed unto him for righteousness, but that his *act of believing* was imputed for righteousness.

In his book *The Cost of Discipleship* Dietrich Bonhoeffer links faith and obedience. Anything less than this close relationship he describes as "cheap grace." To claim God's forgiveness means that we "work through" our sins at the cross. By this is meant that once we understand the cost to God of forgiving our sins, we can never again take sin lightly. This stands in contrast to the position of liberalism described by Richard Niebuhr "that a God without wrath brought men without sin into a kingdom without judgment through the ministration of a Christ without a cross." Actually, forgiveness sets people free to face the issues of life with honesty. The emphasis on the obedience aspect of faith corrects the one-sided emphasis on justification and calls us to sanctification, to wholeness.

When centered in Christ the relationship between faith and conduct is united, and the tension between evangelical proclamation and evangelical service is removed. It is correct to proclaim that the evangel calls people to active obedience, and it is through Christian conduct that the proclamation of the 83 evangel is authenticated. As Jesus made known the kingdom of God by both word and deed (Acts 1:1), so his followers must join word and deed. Our words interpret our deeds, and the deeds authenticate the words. The words articulate the meaning, while the deeds demonstrate the meaning. John Mackay, having served as a Presbyterian missionary and as president of Princeton Theological Seminary, has said that "the two greatest symbols of the Church are the cross and the towel. The one means salvation, the other service. One cannot be had without the other."

In November of 1973, my wife, Esther, and I, along with our three children, were among those who gathered in Chicago at a conference of evangelicals for social action. Here the group drew up and approved the "Declaration of Evangelical Social Concern," defining evangelicalism and expressing the need for a critical consciousness. The following excerpt captures the spirit of the declaration:

> We acknowledge that God requires justice. But we have not proclaimed or demonstrated his justice to an unjust American society. Although the Lord calls us to defend the social and economic rights of the poor and the oppressed, we have mostly remained silent. We deplore the historic involvement of the church in America with racism and the conspicuous responsibility of the evangelical community for perpetuating the personal attitudes and institutional structures that have divided the body of Christ along color lines. Further, we have failed to condemn the exploitation of racism at home and abroad by our economic system . . . . We acknowledge our Christian responsibility of citizenship. Therefore, we must challenge the misplaced trust of the nation in economic and military might—a proud trust that promotes a national pathology

84

of war and violence which victimizes our neighbors at home and abroad. We must resist the temptation to make the nation and its institutions objects of near-religious loyalty.

Faith is an act of identity. Paul, in the sixth chapter of Romans, stresses the in-depth aspects of our identity with Christ. As Søren Kierkegaard, the Danish philosopher and theologian, said, "Faith is passion"; it is the total identification of oneself with Christ. And this relation with Christ moves from the indicative that we are "a new creation" (II Cor. 5:17) to the imperative to be "the new self" (Eph. 4:24). It is this identification with Christ that makes us new creatures; we have a new Lord, a new relationship, a new purpose and motivation, new principles, and new priorities. The source or center of motivation has been changed. We can now speak of the ethic of the new creature, the ethic of the regenerate. There is an ethical aspect to wholeness, to being true to the essential elements of the new relationship with Christ.

We can understand this better by thinking of the Christian life-style as one of fellowship with God before thinking of it in terms of how it is expressed in behavior. God's grace initiates in the believer a change in belonging, then in being, and finally in behaving. The belonging and the being aspects come first. This marvelous fellowship in grace calls forth the ethical aspects of spirit over flesh, of love over selfishness, of righteousness over carnality, of an interdependence with God's people over individualism. It accepts the task of cultural criticism and embraces the biblical imperatives of love, peace, justice, and mutual aid. Knowing the freedom of Christ, the believer is   85 called by the ethic of this new order to work for the freedom and self-fulfillment of all persons.

Obedience is an attitude of fidelity. God claims us wholly, not merely our outward acts. Obedience begins as an inner attitude of faithfulness to God's will. This brings unity and wholeness to the self. In contrast, disobedience is a lack of wholeness, for one is divided and can be one thing now, and then be another. Obedience as wholeness has to do with the disciplines of the inner life, including the clarity with which we discern values, establish priorities, and make choices. It is only when we are obedient that we give evidence of recognizing God's will as the ultimate good. In obedience we are released from selfishness, from the narrow confines of our own wills. But in a far greater way, obedience opens up our lives to the larger possibilities beyond ourselves. The obedient person is a free person.

A pilot, navigating his plane through the air, operates effectively only with a thorough knowledge of the laws of aerodynamics. Only by obeying those laws can the pilot fly. In like manner, the Christian's freedom is secured by obeying God's will.

Obeying involves yielding, which is primarily an affirmation of values. Being motivated by values is transforming, for to speak of existence in love, as Brunner says, "implies the existence of every virtue." To surrender to the divine life beyond oneself is to affirm superior values. This is an experience in humility, but it is the only way we can move from the lesser values to the greater values. "Not my will, but yours be done" (Luke 22:42) is the only avenue to God's greater glory. Yielding is what enables us to share the divine will.

86   Once, when Esther and I were on the island of

Rhodes, we heard the "Light and Sound" presentation of the Knights of St. John. There was an impressive scene when the soldier being knighted was asked, "Do you have the strength to surrender?" That scene often serves to remind me that the integration of faith and conduct calls us as believers to surrender to the mastery of Christ. We thereby model for others the character of Christian conduct, the life of obedience in the grace of Christ. We model the ethic of peace, of the new order, by obedient discipleship. Apart from being disciples of Christ we would only be proponents of a philosophy of life. Jesus calls us to share not just a philosophy, but life itself, his life.

An evangelical ethic of peace will focus on our being disciples of Christ. We confess the historical Jesus as the risen Jesus Christ, as our Lord. To be a disciple of Jesus is to be one who learns from and identifies with the Master. Even so, we do not just follow his teachings on love, peace, or justice—we follow him! New Testament Christianity, as seen in the Gospels, is directly related to the person of Jesus. Discipleship bears witness to him, to Jesus, as Lord. Discipleship identifies with Jesus in all areas of life and engages in a wholistic relationship with him. In this relationship with Jesus, we as Christ's disciples become persons of peace, love, and justice. With these convictions we are given our identity and our vocation. Although many are obsessed with searching for identity, Christ's disciples have already been given their identity.

The term *disciple* is used a total of 260 times in the Gospels and the book of Acts. Luke, in Acts, uses *saint* four times, *Christian* two times, and *disciple* twenty-two times. Scripture teaches that we are not disciples of one another but of Jesus Christ himself, and we become his disciples by our voluntary commitment   87 of faith. This "saving faith" is not a faith that is mystically different from the faith that we normally express in other relationships, for example, faith in friends, in the monetary system, or in a logical conclusion. What makes faith "saving faith" is simply that it is faith placed *in the Savior.* Christ alone reconciles us to God, hence faith in Christ saves us.

As Dietrich Bonhoeffer has said, "Faith only becomes faith in the act of obedience" (*The Cost of Discipleship,* p. 56). And the obedience of faith is in relation to the reign of Jesus, the Christ, who calls us to walk with him, saying, "If anyone would come after me, he must deny himself and take up his cross daily and follow me" (Luke 9:23).

A good definition of discipleship was given by the late dean of Goshen Mennonite Biblical Seminary, Harold Bender, when he spoke of the sixteenth-century Anabaptist movement. He said:

> First and fundamental in the Anabaptist vision was the conception of the essence of Christianity as discipleship. By this was meant the ethical life of radical obedience. This discipleship means the transformation of the entire way of life of the individual believer and of society so that it should be fashioned after the teachings and example of Christ.[3]

Christian discipleship is defined specifically by Kenneth Kinghorn, professor at Asbury Theological Seminary, in four aspects: Discipleship begins with Christ's call to us, it is intensely personal, it requires radical obedience, and it is a way of life. Discipleship is not a Christian legalism, it is the result of our commitment to Jesus. Discipleship is not working to achieve salvation, it is working out the implications

88

of a saving relationship with Jesus. Justification by faith is not curtailed by this understanding of the life of discipleship. The apostle Paul wrote, "Continue to work out your salvation with fear and trembling, for it is God who works in you to will and to act according to his good purpose" (Phil. 2:12*b*-13). God is at work within the life that is open to him. We have been called in grace to enjoy fellowship with Christ, and discipleship is our expression of faithfulness in this relationship. Discipleship concentrates on the concrete manifestation of the Spirit, on following Jesus throughout one's life, a walk described by the Anabaptists as *"Nachfolge Christi."* Hans Denck, a sixteenth-century Anabaptist, expressed it in this way: "No one knows Christ truly unless following Christ daily in life." Jesus taught quite specifically, "By this all men will know that you are my disciples, if you love one another" (John 13:35). Thus, the disciple of Christ has a life-style that finds its model in the Master.

In 1969 it was my privilege to be conference speaker at the various mission conventions across India sponsored by the Evangelical Fellowship of India. At one of those conferences at Landour, in northern India, the associate speaker was Sobod Sahau of Orissa. He told the remarkable story of Sadakar Menon, the nephew of the former minister of defense, Krishna Menon.

Sadakar was a Hindu university student, and he was seeking direction in his life. He went to his favorite philosophy professor at the university, S. Radhakrishnan, who later became the president of India. Sadakar offered to be Radhakrishnan's disciple-servant if the professor would be his guru. To Sadakar's amazement, his Hindu professor said that he was not worthy to be his guru, that only one person in all the world was worthy, and that person was Jesus of Nazareth. 89

Sadakar became angry and replied that Jesus was dead. Sadakar said that he wanted to follow someone who was alive, whom he could walk with, talk with, and learn from. His professor responded, "They say he is alive. I recommend that you get a New Testament and read it."

Sadakar went away angry that day, but later he obtained a New Testament and read it. Through the Holy Spirit's convicting work, Sadakar met the Christ and became a believer. In his new faith he went to a Christian church and was baptized and enrolled in Bible study. Some time later, he returned to the university to talk to his professor. He apologized for having been angry before and said, "I went and got a New Testament and read it. I met the Christ and I've become a Christian."

The Hindu professor reacted by saying, "Oh no, I didn't mean that. You can believe in Jesus and still be a Hindu." But Sadakar said, "No, not the Jesus I have met. He says, 'If anyone would come after me, he must deny himself and take up his cross daily and follow me'" (Luke 9:23). Sadakar Menon later became known as Paul Sadakar, a leading evangelist in India as a disciple of Jesus Christ.

Being a disciple of Christ is a calling of *purpose, priorities,* and *principle.* First, discipleship involves sharing God's *purpose* and ordering one's life by his will. Man's "chief end," the Shorter Catechism of the Westminster Confession says, is "to glorify God and enjoy Him forever." Jesus described his own life with the words, "I have brought you glory on earth by completing the work you gave me to do," (John 17:4). To glorify another is to fully respect the worth and purpose of the other. To glorify God is to let God actually be God in our lives.

90 And as "God was reconciling the world to

himself in Christ" (II Cor. 5:19), believers glorify God by responding to his reconciling grace and by being Christ's disciples. Discipleship presupposes this reconciliation, this new birth and new relationship. And reconciliation, or peace with God, will result in a reconciling peace toward persons around us. Paul wrote, "If it is possible, as far as it depends on you, live at peace with everyone" (Rom. 12:18).

Unfortunately, there is a tendency in evangelical circles to polarize privatistic piety and social ethics. Discipleship is interpreted by some as the humanistic aspect of social concern. This is an inadequate understanding of discipleship. Being a disciple of Jesus is only possible by walking in the Spirit, by identifying with the risen Christ in the most personal way. As friendship is possible only by having a relationship with a friend, so discipleship is possible only by having a relationship with the Master. If we are at peace with Christ, his reconciling peace will govern our relationships with others also.

God's purpose for us is first to be reconciled to Christ, and second, to participate in Christ's kingdom. Jesus spoke specifically of his purpose for his disciples in the Sermon on the Mount, saying, "But seek first his kingdom and his righteousness, and all these things will be given to you as well" (Matt. 6:33). The purpose to which believers are called is to participate fully in God's reign in the kingdom of right relations, a kingdom of the "rule of God" in life. This rule of Jesus is to be the norm for the people of God, for those who are experiencing God's transforming grace.

As disciples of Christ in this kingdom, we move in society aware that "our citizenship [commonwealth] is in heaven" (Phil. 3:20). We are to be in the world but not of the world (see John 15:19). As the light of the world and the salt of the earth, believers are to   91 serve Christ by enriching society. As was emphasized in chapter 2, salt and light benefit what they affect. Church of the Brethren professor and author Vernard Eller once quipped, "We put salt on celery not to admire the salt, but so that the celery will taste 'celerier'." Christians who are the salt of the earth help the world to become more truly the world God intended. Discipleship is therefore something of a corrective agent in society. This is not accomplished by identifying the kingdom of God with a particular society, however; it is carried out by a confronting and enriching proclamation, and by believers being examples of what it means to be under the "rule of Christ" within society.

Further emphasis on this role of the disciple in society has been given by Foy Valentine, a Southern Baptist churchman. He said, "No greater heresy has beset the Christian Church than that which has separated the personal from the social, evangelism from ethics, faith from works, root from branch, words from deeds." As voices of an evangelical faith, Christians must view ethics—the call of a new life-style—as an essential aspect of the gospel, while they aggressively permeate each stratum of society with the gospel. We must also model this new creation as members of a new community of the people of God, which John R. W. Stott calls "a Christian counterculture." As such, we affirm Christ's judgment on social evils, materialisms, individualism, intemperance, selfish sensuality, racial and cultural prejudice, violence and war, and so forth.

W. H. Auden left us some expressive lines:

> The expert designing the long-range gun,
> To exterminate everyone under the sun,
> Would like to get out but can only mutter;—
> "What can I do? It's my bread and butter."

92

We are increasingly aware that as disciples we live in a hostile world. Politically, alienation has for many created a lack of trust in the body politic. Morally, man's "anomie" has increased overt expressions of selfishness. As James Baldwin said in *The Fire Next Time*, "Whoever debases others debases himself." Socially, the world's urban anonymity has contributed to depersonalization, as has man's technology. Not long ago, the computer was honored as *Time* magazine's "Man of the Year." Spiritually, much of the church continues to be morally anemic even while it seeks to renew its piety.

Evangelical Christians need to wrestle squarely with some difficult questions. For example, How do we relate Christian faith and discipleship to a society that thinks itself Christian? How do we make compassionate discipleship visible or recognizable amid our affluence or materialism? How do we make faith in Christ an option for people who think they have all that they need in secularism? These issues confront believers who seek to follow God's purpose as authentic disciples in society.

Discipleship is a matter of purpose but also a matter of *priorities*. In the passage in Luke 9:57-58, a man offered to follow Jesus, so Jesus tested the man's motives with the statement, "Foxes have holes and birds of the air have nests, but the Son of Man has no place to lay his head" (Luke 9:58). The implication was that one becomes a disciple to be with the Master, not for what one can get out of it for oneself.

Discipleship as a matter of priorities has to do with ordering or arranging life patterns. The exercise is itself a value judgment. Setting priorities requires selectivity. One must choose some things over others, and then be able to arrange the choices in proper   93 order. As disciples of Christ we not only give up the "bad" for the "good," but beyond the good we decide between the good, the better, and the best.

Jesus has given us some specific guidance for setting priorities in his teachings on love, righteousness, peace, and equity. In fact, he made love the first priority by saying, "Love the Lord your God with all your heart and with all your soul and with all your mind and with all your strength" (Mark 12:30, 31). Love for God followed by love for neighbor is the foundation of peace.

Setting priorities that correspond to God's priorities is a basic expression of discipleship. It is in this way that faith becomes visible. In Jesus' words, "Love your neighbor as yourself," there is a strategy to change the world. We are to learn to treat enemies as brothers and sisters rather than treat brothers and sisters as enemies. Jesus' teaching that we are to turn the other cheek is to be the disciples' strategy; it makes faith in him visible to the world. It is only with this approach that we as disciples do not let our actions be determined by how others treat us; rather, we are free to act on the basis of another principle. This strategy works not only interpersonally, but can transform social and international relations. We should live by the highest standards of our own beliefs rather than let the behavior of others determine our actions. Such a command from Jesus for ethical norms is imperative for his disciples.

Establishing Christian priorities expresses a value system that takes the will of God seriously. It is taking positive action rather than being first a negative discipline. As was said earlier, one's yes to God should have priority over one's no. In ethical decisions one seeks the positive acts that express the reign of God and in so doing, one follows a vocation of enriching, creative love.

94

My wife, Esther, is an artist. She and I have discussed and wrestled at length with the issue of the theology of art. We fully appreciate creativity as a feature of our partnership with the Creator, reflecting God's image in us, but we believe that to make creativity an end in itself is actually to become an anti-creator, to stand over against God. The aesthetic expression can be enjoyed as a humanistic experience, but aesthetic expressions can be enjoyed better as worship experiences that engage our higher personhood in partnership with God. The disciple sees all of life in relation to the Master, the Lord of (and in) creation.

In Luke 9, Jesus invited a man to follow him (v. 59). This man replied, "Lord, first let me go and bury my father." The man meant that he needed to carry on his father's business until the father died, and then the son could come and be Christ's disciple. There is clearly a question of priorities here. Jesus' answer, "Let the dead bury their own dead, but you go and proclaim the kingdom of God" (v. 60), could be paraphrased, "Let that which is a part of the dying order of the age die, but give yourself to the qualities and actions of eternal life."

Discipleship has purpose and priorities, but it also has *principles*. Discipleship as a life of principle means above all that Christians relate to a person, the Master, not to systems of thought or religion. But relationships between persons have their own principles of humility, honesty, integrity, faithfulness, love, equity, justice, peace, and so forth. These principles guide us in our walk with the Master at the same time that they are aspects of the relationship itself.

The ethic of this new order of discipleship is expressed by Jesus not in petty rules, but in principles of love, equity, peace, and righteousness. Paul expressed this in the book of Romans: "For the   95 kingdom of God is not a matter of eating and drinking, but of righteousness, peace and joy in the Holy Spirit" (Rom. 14:17). Christian ethics offers answers, but not in neat outlines that can be followed by rote. Detailed proof-texting of issues treats the Scriptures like an encyclopedia, but misses the larger scriptural principles by which believers are to make ethical decisions. It is by applying biblical principles to our decision making that we mature. Decisions make the most of the positive aspects of development. Decisions of faith keep us growing in the positive dimensions of Christlikeness rather than developing a legalism of detailed perfor- mance. It is in this spirit that J. B. Phillips said, "The failure to do good to people in need is just as sinful as to do them harm."

German theologian Emil Brunner has said, "The Christian is never called to act on *general principles* but always in accordance with the concrete commandment of love" (emphasis added). Deciding to act in such loving ways promotes our maturity. Adam and Eve were created innocent but immature, for maturity comes through making decisions. Even so, when the time came for decision making, they made wrong decisions and failed to mature in godliness. In contrast, Jesus, the last Adam, made right decisions, and, as we read in Hebrews, was made mature (perfect) by the things he suffered (see Heb. 5:8-9).

Looking again at Luke 9, we note a third person in the dialogue on discipleship. This was the man who offered to follow Jesus but wanted first to go back and have a farewell party with his family and friends. Following Jesus, however, is not to be treated as a casual excursion into some different role; it is a total commitment to the person and will of Christ. Jesus 96 said, "No one who puts his hand to the plow and looks back is fit for service in the kingdom of God" (Luke 9:62). A call to discipleship is a call to integrity, to faithfulness in one's commitment to Christ. Above all, it is a call to live by the principles of the kingdom of God.

An emphasis on a relationship with Christ as our highest principle must be seen in the larger dimensions of covenant. By covenant I mean a mutually binding commitment. This is not just an existential togetherness, it is a covenant of fidelity. When he instituted the Lord's supper, Jesus described the elements as symbols of the new covenant, saying, "This is my body given for you," and, "This cup is the new covenant in my blood" (Luke 22:19-20). Jesus made these statements while he was still in his earthly body, his blood flowing in his veins. Yet he was saying by the elements that his covenant was a pledge to the death for the disciples and for all believers (see also Mark 14:22-25). Thus, our sharing this covenant relationship should be a pledge to the death on our part for Christ. This covenant of faithfulness is the ethic of the new order. We do not claim salvation in the grace of Christ and then continue to live by selfish choices. Discipleship involves yielding, submitting to Jesus as Master. To receive salvation is to enter into a covenant relationship with Christ, becoming his disciples.

Jesus said, "Whoever acknowledges me before men, I will also acknowledge him before my Father in heaven" (Matt. 10:32). And Paul wrote that "if you confess with your mouth, 'Jesus is Lord,' and believe in your heart that God raised him from the dead, you will be saved" (Rom. 10:9). John expressed the same truth: "But if we walk in the light, as he is in the light, we have fellowship with one another, and the blood of Jesus, his Son, purifies [keeps cleansing] us from every sin" (I John 1:7). The Greek language used in these 97 passages makes clear that walking in the light is a continuing practice. As believers walk in this covenant relation, the blood of Jesus continues to cleanse them from sin.

Indeed, discipleship cannot exist outside of this covenant relationship with Christ. Mennonite professor and educator Laurence Burkholder says of the Anabaptist approach to ethics: "Biblical command and direct obedience take place within the church, the body of Christ, and under the direction of the Holy Spirit." This is to say that Christian ethics is expected only of committed Christians, for Christian conduct issues from a vital experience of faith.

Discipleship, then, begins by our deciding to be in a saving-faith relationship with Jesus and continues with commitment to him. The dynamic change that results from a deep commitment to Christ is illustrated in the story of the life of Marian Preminger. Born in Hungary in 1913, Marian was raised in a castle with all of the privileges of royalty. While attending school in Vienna, Marian fell in love with a doctor and they eloped; however, the marriage lasted only one year. Later, while auditioning for a play, she met a brilliant young German director, Otto Preminger. They fell in love, married, and later moved to America. Marian then got caught up in a sensual life in Hollywood, and her second husband divorced her.

Marian returned to Europe, where she became a prominent socialite in Paris, but, with a vast emptiness in her life, she had a longing for peace. Hearing that Albert Schweitzer was in Europe, she was able to arrange to see him. They met at the village church where he was playing the organ, and she turned pages for him while he played. After having dinner with

98 him, she discovered what she regarded as God's

answer to her life's quest, the calling to serve Christ. As a consequence, Marian went to Africa and worked in the Albert Schweitzer Hospital at Lambarene, where she cared for babies, fed lepers, and changed bandages.

When it carried her obituary in 1979, the *New York Times* printed Marian Preminger's words, quoted from Albert Schweitzer: "There are two classes of people in the world, the helpers and the non-helpers. I'm a helper." It is Christ who truly enables us to be "helpers," disciples who share his ministry of reconciliation.

NOTES

1. Emil Brunner, *The Divine Imperative* (Philadelphia: Westminster Press, 1960), pp. 135-36.
2. John Howard Yoder, *The Legacy of Sattler* (Scottdale, Pa.: Herald Press, 1973), p. 123.
3. Laurence Burkholder, "Ethics," vol. 4 of *Mennonite Encyclopedia* (Scottdale, Pa.: Mennonite Pub. House, 1955), p. 1080.

COVENANT COMMUNITY AND FREEDOM

6 An ethic of peace is to be modeled by the community of believers. Note Paul's words: "For he himself is our peace, who has made the two one and has destroyed the barrier, the dividing wall of hostility" (Eph. 2:14). The source of the Christian's ethic of peace is God's act of grace in Christ. Through this act, Christ has reconciled us to God and, in turn, to one another.

The heart of the gospel is God's act of reconciliation in Christ. This is the meaning of salvation by grace, that God took the initiative and came to us. God's yes is as large as the cross, as large as Christ, as large as the resurrection. God's yes means that he is completely open to us, inviting our yes in response.

The ethic of peace is not an ethic that is expected of society in general, but is an ethic for the regenerate, for the members of the body of Christ. God is creating within society a reconciled community, a community of believers to live in freedom and fellowship. In this new community we as believers are to model the way of peace. This consciousness-raising model will expose the perversions in society so that persons will be encouraged to seek the fellowship of Christ. The new community is to demonstrate the true meaning of peace, love, and justice in human relations. We are ethically responsible for expressing the very nature of Jesus, whose life demonstrated the love of God for all persons, including the enemies of God. 101

To be reconciled is to be restored, not just to a place, but to a relationship. Reconciliation introduces the One who is wholly other and yet who has come to us in Jesus of Nazareth. In Jesus "the Word became flesh and made his dwelling among us. We have seen his glory, the glory of the One and Only, who came from the Father" (John 1:14). Christ Jesus of Nazareth was truly human without being sinful. Hence the Incarnation, God as human, shows us that humanness and sinfulness are not synonymous.

As Christians, our reconciliation to God through Christ is a restoration: "To all who received him, to those who believed in his name, he gave the right to become children of God" (John 1:12). Since by God's act of creation we were made in the very image of God, we understand this *Imago Dei* to be the character of true humanness. Through our sin against God this *Imago Dei* has been perverted, for our sinfulness is a perversion of the good in which we were created. But our salvation, our being regenerated, is above all a reconciliation with God, and as such it re-creates the *Imago Dei*—re-creates what it means to be truly human. In Christ we are new creatures, the kind of persons God wants us to be, truly human. And God's reconciliation re-creates this true humanity.

On the other hand, this humanness, or humanism, that reconciliation makes possible is to be distinguished from secularism. The word *humanism* should be reserved for its higher meaning: humanity as God intended it to be. For some people, *humanism* is a dangerous word; yet in my opinion, who has more of a right to use the word than the people of God, who are people of the new order and members of his kingdom of the reconciled? Having been

102

reconciled to God through the cross, in the Christ who is "our peace," we are now agents of reconciliation in relation to all others in society.

We as Christians are reconciled, a new people created in and for community. No one is complete alone. The fullness of life can only be found in relationships. This is first realized in our relationship with God, and it is authenticated in relationships with others. Such is the community of believers in which the meaning of reconciling love is to be expressed. In the story of creation, God made man and woman alike in his image. That is to say, he created them in and for community, to have fellowship with one another and with God.

The new community is expressed in covenant. This covenant is a mutual commitment, creating a community of love, and is a relationship based on trust. It is built on nothing less than Christ's blood—his "blood of the covenant," which was his pledge to the death for us. This is the foundation of a new relationship, one that includes our covenant to the death for Christ. The cross is the cost of the new order of grace that is now.

This new community is composed both of the forgiven and the forgiving. Forgiveness is liberating. It involves acceptance, but it also effects release. Forgiveness results in a refusal by a person to seek to control another, a refusal to manipulate another, a refusal to enter into a power play that controls others by filling them with feelings of guilt. Forgiveness is an act of love. It is the restoring of a relationship rather than remaining aloof. God has forgiven us in Christ.

This new community of the forgiven and the forgiving is thus a community of freedom, and freedom is necessary for peace. While peace brings harmony to one's inner spirit, it also expresses 103 one's respect for another. Peace enhances the well-being of each person and increases each person's potential for development and achievement.

Forgiveness is of God. Only God can fully see beyond the issue to the person; only God can fully accept and affirm the dignity of each person. The community of the reconciled understands forgiveness, for it is only by God's forgiving grace that disciples of Christ are made a community together. In turn, such a community, when true to its cause, will extend forgiveness to others. The community of the reconciled is consequently a liberating community. To forgive another is to believe that a person's life is more than the sum of the mistakes that have been made. To forgive is to believe that a person can be changed, that although one has failed, one can rise again by the grace of God. Forgiveness initiates an inner change, a change in the person forgiven, for reconciling peace brings harmony to the person's spirit. The new experience of love will now be expressed in freedom, the freedom of restored relationships.

Forgiveness is hard, because it is required of the innocent, who is suffering for the guilty. Forgiveness involves resolving one's wrath on the sin of another with love, so that without humiliation, one lets the other go free. When we forgive, persons are liberated without being made to crawl, because we reflect in our own spirit the meaning of Jesus' words, "Father, forgive them, for they do not know what they are doing" (Luke 23:34).

We are enabled in the reconciled community to transcend selfishness and individualism. In fact, true community takes place only with diversity, not without it. It is only in diversity itself that genuine community can be expressed, for then the

104

oneness in faith is demonstrated that respects the differences of our individuality. The agape ethic seeks the well-being of our partners, so that a Christian community becomes a liberating community. This freedom in the fellowship of Christ seeks to make the most of the potential of each person, for in freedom we enable one another to achieve the wholeness that God intends for each one.

Christian ethics calls us to look first within ourselves, rather than at circumstances or situations beyond ourselves. James writes,

> What causes fights and quarrels among you? Don't they come from your desires that battle within you? You want something but don't get it. You kill and covet, but you cannot have what you want. You quarrel and fight. You do not have, because you do not ask God. When you ask, you do not receive, because you ask with wrong motives, that you may spend what you get on your pleasures. (James 4:1-3)

Samuel Shoemaker, famous Episcopal rector of New York and Pittsburgh, has said that war is simply the problem of human selfishness written large.

From another perspective, pride is our basic sin as humans. One does not overcome pride simply by a monastic exercise of self-humiliation. Rather, in positive acts of service to others, we are enabled to transcend self-interests. It is these positive acts that make for peace and freedom in the community of the reconciled.

As disciples of Christ, we are called to give and to receive correction in this new community. We thereby hold each other accountable to the will of God as revealed in Scripture. Several difficult   105 chapters in the writings of the apostle Paul, including Romans 14 and I Corinthians 8, deal with relationships in which Christians have differing consciences. In these passages Paul makes clear that "none of us lives to himself alone and none of us dies to himself alone" (Rom. 14:7). In this context we are taught not to judge the motives of our companions, but to leave this judgment to God. Further, we are told that we should be careful "not to put any stumbling block or obstacle in [our] brother's way" (Rom. 14:13). However, Paul leads us in a more positive direction when he says, "Let us therefore make every effort to do what leads to peace and to mutual edification" (Rom. 14:19). These teachings must also be read alongside Paul's statements on the disciplined church, in I Corinthians 5 and II Corinthians 2. Paul emphasizes in those passages the believer's responsibility for holding another accountable before God, and teaches that such discipline enhances our consistency in our walk with God.

In Matthew 18:15-18, Jesus clearly said how we are to give and receive correction within the community of believers. It is incumbent upon us ethically to help one another conduct ourselves according to the will of Christ, while it is also true that church discipline is important for the sake of a good witness to the society in which the church stands. When members of the reconciled community fail to practice the discipleship that they confess, the community of believers is responsible for holding them accountable and helping them to achieve the walk of faith that will enrich their own lives and that of the community. This approach to discipline contrasts directly with the patterns of our western individualism, and with the attitudes of those whose life-styles are more existential, who 106 operate on the basis of practicing whatever appears good to them. The discipline of being in a caring community that gives and receives rebuke is essential to our maturing in ethical discernment, and enhances our discipline and personal wholeness.

To "hold one another accountable" is not to be reduced to a form of legalism where we become guardians of one another's morality. Rather, this accountability is a matter of fellowship in the freedom of the Spirit, where the openness in our fellowship is constantly enriched. Although it is costly, transparency before God and one another is important for mental and emotional health. This transparency is reflected in the honesty and integrity with which the people of God share with one another in the fellowship of Christ. Peter writes:

> But you are a chosen people, a royal priesthood, a holy nation, a people belonging to God, that you may declare the praises of him who called you out of darkness into his wonderful light. Once you were not a people, but now you are the people of God; once you had not received mercy, but now you have received mercy. (I Pet. 2:9, 10)

It is in the liberty of being God's people that we are granted freedom in our relationships with one another.

Further, reconciliation with God means that as Christians we are reconciled to all that God is doing in the world. Reconciliation defines the term *justification by faith* and both terms, *reconciliation* and *justification*, should be seen in this order rather than the other way around. In the western world especially, justification by faith has been emphasized individualistically. In contrast, when we see that reconciliation provides the content for justification by faith, 107 we will obviously get involved in the social aspects as well as the personal aspects of faith. Too often the emphasis on justification and assurance of salvation has remained a private religion, even amid pietistic and charismatic movements. Though this pious religion may be beautifully expressed in devotional exercises, either alone or with persons of a similar religion who gather to worship, it may fail to apply the meaning of faith to the whole of life. Reconciliation calls us into a justifying faith-relation with God and consequently with all that God is doing in society.

A community of the redeemed is a liberating community. It bases its decisions on whether an act enhances or limits the freedom of Christ in the group. This is not "situationism," which is hardly a self-sufficient position in Christian ethics. There are moral limits. We make day-to-day decisions on the basis of our understanding of, and commitment to, Jesus Christ. Christ himself stands as the norm for personhood and for interpersonal relations. One does not isolate agape love from the person of Christ, or talk about an agape ethic, without seeing the content for that agape in the person and holiness of Jesus himself.

Professor John C. Bennett of New York speaks of this in his book *The Radical Imperative* in a critique of ethicist Joseph Fletcher:

> The danger of situationism in recognizing no limits in principle to what is morally permissible can be well seen in what is to me an extraordinary passage in Fletcher's *Situation Ethics*. He says that on a vast scale of agapeic calculus President Truman made his decision about the A Bomb on Hiroshima and Nagasaki. If such a direct massacre of a civilian population

108

is consistent with agape, I fail to see that there are any limits to the deeds of horror that can be permitted in its name.[1]

The church, or the community of the reconciled, is committed to the agape ethic. Consequently, it is called to confront even the political systems with its witness to a higher ethic. The church is called to model in society the meaning of living in the will of Christ, and thereby speak to the conscience of those in the political and social structures that influence the life and freedoms of society. Our witness as members of this community is to call on the government to practice to the utmost the ethics called for by the constitution of the government and the governed. At the same time, the church's witness in any society should serve to raise that ethical perception to the highest extent possible for that social order.

In summary, the community of the reconciled is, through the regeneration of the Spirit, granted the ability to live in love (Rom. 5:5). In turn, it is called to commit itself to being active in loving, in acts of compassion. This is a community of people committed to mutually responsible action in support and enrichment of one another. The Christian community owes its highest loyalty to Jesus Christ and his kingdom. It is free to critique itself, and thereby to interrupt the cycle that would move it toward institutionalism. It is free to critique society and expose society's goals to fulfill itself without God. It is free to critique the state and judge what is acceptable, and what is of Caesar and against God in the idolatry of power. It is free to critique materialism and to expose the idolatry of material power in the disproportionate acquisition of resources. The demands of such a community are high: It is easy to be a materialist, an idealist, a Commu-   109 nist, or even an anti-Communist, for those individuals leave decisions on morals to subjective judgments. On the other hand, to be a community of disciples of Christ is demanding, for it means holding one another accountable to his will.

Such a community is only possible by the transforming grace of Christ, mediated to us by the Holy Spirit. In the midst of our doctrinal defensiveness regarding the social implications of the evangelical gospel, we need a more creative movement of liberated evangelicals. Such a movement will expect and participate in the fresh, creative movements of the Spirit. Such a movement will espouse a "third way," the way of the reconciled, of the kingdom of Christ. This "third way" of the kingdom frees those whose philosophical and cultural stance is to the right or to the left. Those who seek to follow the "third way" will take seriously the role of the Spirit in the stream of history. The community of disciples will identify with acceptable conservative values from that stream without being locked into a conservative system of life and thought.

Followers of the "third way" will also recognize new, creative ways to use the truth of Christ in confronting the issues of our time. Enabled by the spirit, the community of disciples will at times identify with acceptable liberal values without being locked into liberalism. Evangelicals of the "third way" will be selective in the world, basing their decisions on the kingdom of Christ, which is the kingdom of the reconciled. Such disciples will live by an ethic of peace and work for peace.

The testimony of faith in the believing community is its own "test" of success. Years ago a bedraggled student of Columbia University in

New York City walked the streets all night, wrestling with his inner doubts about a personal God who gives meaning to life. On Sunday morning he slipped into a church and sat and listened to the service. At the time of prayer, he didn't bow his head but simply looked around the room. He was surprised to see one of his favorite professors reverently bowed in prayer, worshiping. The student thought, "If that man, as a great scientist, believes in God, I can look at faith again." Years later, while on furlough from missionary service in India, he went and looked up his onetime professor, who was by then an old man. He told his professor what had happened to him that Sunday morning, and he thanked him for his silent influence of faith. The covenant community, living in reconciliation with God, will have this kind of pervasive influence on all of life.

NOTES

1. John C. Bennett, *The Radical Imperative* (Philadelphia: Westminster Press, 1975), p. 48.

111

The Centrality of Love

7 Love is the giving of oneself for the benefit and enrichment of another. Love is not an objective; it is the spirit in which we live. This love calls us to integrity, to wholeness that can be trusted, which is essential to peacemaking. It is by God's love that we are called into the new community of God's people, into a relation of covenant. And there is no covenant of love without integrity on the part of the "covenantors." In the Old Testament we read that blessing is "because the Lord loved you and kept the oath he swore to your forefathers" (Deut. 7:8). In this passage we see that God's love is the basis for his call of grace.

What place does love have in an ethic of peace? Love is the activity, the conduct we as disciples of Christ are called to as peacemakers. According to the Anabaptist perspective in the Radical Reformation, the central idea of the Christian ethic is love. This position holds that the full meaning of love is known supremely in Christ's sacrificial death on the cross, and the Christian ethic therefore starts with self-giving by believers as they follow their Lord's model. To be peacemakers then means that we as Christians begin by surrendering selfish ambition and living by nonresistant love.

The way of love in peacemaking is not passive, it is an active expression of self-giving. We must clearly distinguish between passiveness and pacifism. The depth of the love of Christ was displayed on the cross, whereon he confronted human injustice 113 with redemptive grace by expressing the true character of aggressive pacificism. To love as Jesus loves is to use whatever powers we have to serve others. Agape love is not so much an affection as an attitude of the will.

Love is assertive, in that it continually moves God to be involved in our experience. This same assertiveness led Jesus to drive the venders from the temple and call for it to be restored as a place of prayer for all nations. Jesus did not ignore the venders' schemes, which barred the Gentiles from admission to the court for worship. In love, Jesus not only called those venders to face their condition, he also held them accountable for making just decisions for all others influenced by those decisions.

Love is difficult, for it involves risk, a total self-giving. In fact, one has not come to understand deep love until one has died to selfishness for the sake of serving others. It is in the experience of dying to self-centeredness that one is opened to the new freedom offered by Jesus Christ. Indeed, there is a psychological release when one has faced this aspect of death and is thereby delivered from the fear of death. One can now live by the principles of love and nonviolence. But in order to experience that release, the cause for which one dies must be the greater cause of the will of God and the well-being of humanity.

Love does recognize the existence of moral dilemmas. Some of the most difficult questions in life are those that focus on what the course of love should be when a moral dilemma offers no way out of a situation unless someone suffers. Such moral dilemmas confront the Christian in the realm of the sinfulness of this world. Here God judges us by our motives, whether what we do is with the intent of working for the glory of God and the "shalom," or well-being, of others.

An ethic for a Christian life-style includes the orders of our common life. In fact, faith in practice becomes a visible witness to the larger society. Jesus said, "By this all men will know that you are my disciples, if you love one another" (John 13:35). In Jesus' prayer in John 17, he states that the oneness in which we are together in Christ, as he is in God, enables the world to understand the reality of the gospel of grace.

The way of love modeled by the church becomes a witness to society, and this witness calls society to more venerable behavior than would be true or possible if the Christian model were not present to speak to society's conscience. People behave better when they are given something excellent to compete with, even if they do not accept it for themselves. It is in this regard that the witness of love, peace, and justice on the part of the Christian community should enable society to wrestle with higher principles than those that characterize the general humanistic commitment. But too often the church lowers its standards to those of its social environment.

Our witness for peace is especially relevant in a day of nuclear armament and the possibilities of global suicide. Thousands of warheads exist more than fifty times stronger than the atomic bomb that obliterated Hiroshima. Thus, global suicide is actually possible. The National Security Council in the United States estimates that in a nuclear war, 140 million Americans and 100 million Russians would die in the opening few minutes. Books on the dangers of nuclear war have proliferated in the last several years. *The Day After,* the ABC television program on the holocaust of a nuclear war, which aired on November 20, 1983, was an appeal to the American conscience to think and act responsibly before a mushroom cloud rises.   115

One sign of hope is the heightened awareness in society of the potential devastation. This awareness has led some members of society to protest, to appeal for communication that confronts political leaders with the need for ceasing the nuclear arms build-up, and to seek the reallocation of monies to meet human needs. As Senator Edward Kennedy said at Liberty Baptist College, "There is no morality in a mushroom cloud."

Whether what we are doing in the nuclear arms race is consistent with agape love in meeting human need is a question that can be answered by the secularist as well as by the Christian. Secularists would more readily believe in Christ if they saw us modeling his love. We need to rediscover that to "love your neighbor as yourself" (Mark 12:31) is a strategy that can change the world. Carnal weapons can only destroy; it takes loving action to build and enrich the human family.

Both the Old and New Testaments call us to the first commandment, to love God with all of the heart, soul, mind, and strength. The Old and New Testaments alike call us to love our neighbors as ourselves, a teaching that Jesus identified as the second commandment, of the same nature and quality as the first commandment. What is unique about Jesus' teachings in this regard is that they extend the meaning of "neighbor" to include all persons, both friends and enemies. Adopting this attitude can change the social orders of the world. Jesus specifically taught his disciples to love their enemies. As believers, we too are called to treat enemies as friends rather than as enemies.

Jesus' words still stand before us: "Put your sword back in its place . . . for all who draw the sword will die by the sword" (Matt. 26:52). In his book *What Would You Do?* John Howard Yoder sets before

116

us a theological discussion and examples from life of the way of love and nonviolence in human relations.[1] In essence he shows that although love is costly, it does not have to win to succeed. Love by its very expression enriches any society.

One of Jesus' remarkable statements on love is found in the Gospel of Luke, chapter 6, verses 27-36:

> But I tell you who hear me: Love your enemies, do good to those who hate you, bless those who curse you, pray for those who mistreat you. If someone strikes you on one cheek, turn to him the other also. If someone takes your cloak, do not stop him from taking your tunic. Give to everyone who asks you, and if anyone takes what belongs to you, do not demand it back. Do to others as you would have them do to you. If you love those who love you, what credit is that to you? Even 'sinners' love those who love them. And if you do good to those who are good to you, what credit is that to you? Even 'sinners' do that. And if you lend to those from whom you expect repayment, what credit is that to you? Even 'sinners' lend to 'sinners,' expecting to be repaid in full. But love your enemies, do good to them, and lend to them without expecting to get anything back. Then your reward will be great, and you will be sons of the Most High, because he is kind to the ungrateful and wicked. Be merciful, just as your Father is merciful.

Jesus teaches in this passage that *love elevates others above oneself.* His teaching on loving our enemies is simply that we should extend our love and interest to conform to God's love and interest, which encompasses all persons. We are told by Jesus to love our enemies, that is, not to look out for ourselves but to care for them.

This love is also morally discerning and carries with it a hatred of evil. Love knows the

117

harm that evil brings to persons, and it seeks to deal with this harm. Genuine love is not sentimental, it is morally strong, and it is demonstrated by praying for other persons, thereby seeking their well-being in relation to God.

In Luke 6:29, Christ tells us that when we are buffeted, we are to turn the other cheek. To do so is not to surrender, it is rather the Christian strategy for operating, for it is in the very act of turning the other cheek that we demonstrate our freedom. We have been liberated in Jesus Christ so that rather than have our behavior toward another individual determined by his or her treatment of us, we can live by other convictions. When we turn the other cheek we demonstrate that our behavior is determined by our choice to obey Christ rather than by the human tendency to react in the same way we have been treated.

Paul also makes clear in Romans 12 and 13 that love does not return evil for evil. Paul's teaching sounds like an echo of the Sermon on the Mount, especially Romans 12:14-19. To curse people is to wish them evil. To do them good is to serve them and to seek their well-being. Love is positive. As a consequence, both Jesus and Paul teach that retaliation and revenge are ruled out by love.

Love in a real sense is a conquest of evil (Rom. 12:20-21). Here Paul is teaching us that the enemy can be overcome by good, that vengeance is to be replaced by service. When Paul writes that if our enemies hunger, we should feed them, we should understand that this is done not to embarrass the persons, but to help reclaim them for fellowship. Martin Luther King wrote from the jail cell to his people, "Love your enemies. Not only do we refuse to increase the evil by our responses, but we will diminish the evil when those pursuing evil are won over to goodness." The old adage is appropriate here: "To return evil for good is devilish, to return good for good or evil for evil is human, but to return good for evil is divine."

Paul's strategy of overcoming evil with good is a way of Christian action in the midst of social conflict. Sociologist Max Weber said, "Conflict cannot be excluded from social life . . . . Peace is nothing more than a change in the form 'of the conflict' or in the antagonist or in the objects of the conflict, or finally in the changes of selection."[2] The way of love does not deny conflict, nor does it ignore it; rather, love is a strategy for working in situations of conflict with respect for all of the persons engaged in the conflict. Love is not passive in its nonviolence, it is actively engaged in overcoming the evil of the conflict with the good of reconciliation, of nonviolent association.

Jesus further teaches us that *love elevates persons above the material.* One of the basic causes of tension between persons arises from the misuse of one another. When it is clear that we seek the well-being of each other, this in itself promotes peace in relationships. Jesus says that we are always to regard the person as more important than the material. He instructs us to give to the one who is destitute, to lend to the person in need—policies that enable the recipient not only to save face but to develop a greater sense of worth in return.

Deeds of love do not mean that we compromise principles that hold us accountable to each other. A loving deed is not a gift to be given that then allows us to end our relationship with the needy person. The act of love involves us with the persons in need; we help such persons by holding them accountable and by enabling them to learn the disciplines and   119 principles of management that will help them succeed. For instance, a church may place funds in a bank as an account providing security for persons who lack credit references. These persons can then borrow from the bank, meet payment schedules, and build their own credit references. Similarly, in Romans 12, the apostle Paul outlines the course of action in love with the goal of rehabilitating persons and restoring relationships.

The theology of reconciliation is based on God's act in Christ to reconcile us to himself (II Cor. 5:19). God did not simply offer us some benefit to meet a particular need, he offered himself in continuing fellowship. Just so, the action of love elevates persons above the material, refuses to measure the cost in dollars, but rather measures it by what it means for the well-being of the persons served.

When persons are elevated above the material there is no justification for violence or for the destruction of another person for the sake of our material interests. Such a stance is contrary to the human spirit, for it causes us to become judges of others. It causes us to become violent in our spirits, rather than seeking to discover in Christ how to love others as an extension of our loving God.

Love is to be experienced personally, but also socially and politically. Retired General Robert Mathias spoke at the Pasadena, California, conference in May 1983. In his speech, entitled "The Church and Peacemaking in the Nuclear Age," he shared his own struggle with the issues of love and nonviolence. General Mathias said in his presentation that it is imperative that we as Christians struggle with the issues of nuclear warfare and chemical warfare, but we must also recognize that killing persons with a 30-caliber rifle equally violates the will of God. In this same conference, Bill Pannel of Fuller Seminary asked, "What would happen if the gospel worked and called the saints to be peacemakers beyond ideology?"

Jesus' teaching on elevating persons above the material calls us to recognize the supreme value of human life, of personality. God's creation of life, and the gift of humanness, are to be fully respected. This means that there is need for a stronger consciousness of the evil of abortion and of safeguarding the life of the unborn; but this must also be balanced with a consciousness of the right to life of the already born, and a commitment to safeguard the life and well-being of all people. As Ron Sider, in Ghandian terms, stated at the Pasadena Conference on Peacemaking, "I am willing to die to protect democratic freedom, but I am not willing to kill for it." In an article entitled "An Evangelical's Concern About Evangelical Unconcern" (*Minister's Personal Library Journal*, Vol. III, No. 3, 1982), Vernon Grounds, former president of Denver Theological Seminary, called for an awakened conscience among evangelicals on the right-to-life for all people:

> What about the schizophrenia of people who cry out against the murder of embryonic babies yet refuse to cry out against wholesale murder by atomic bombs? For the use of nuclear weapons will indiscriminately kill millions of incalculably precious persons, including, no doubt, at least a few million babies! In my judgment, consequently, the same judgment which motivates the evangelical battle against abortion as an evil that destroys human life ought to motivate an impassioned anti-nuclear crusade. To denounce one evil while condoning the other is surely schizophrenic.

Jesus also teaches us that in *love we elevate behavior above bargaining.* In Luke 6, Christ   121 shows us that it is not what we get out of our deeds, but rather what happens in the interchange that enables each of us to be truly human. We have been created in the image of God, and we are fulfilled when we live in a manner consistent with that image. Our hospitality, our deeds of charity, our activities in any area of loving service, are to grow out of agape love. Such love does not ask what it will receive in return. "God so loved the world that he gave his one and only Son"—to the extent of death on the cross, without asking for benefits in return. Human nature on the other hand tends to ask, What's in it for me?

In the context of Romans 12 and 13, the apostle Paul raises the issue of how Christian love conducts itself in relation to political authorities. We will deal with ethics and the political questions in another chapter. For now, it is important to see how Paul joins love and Christian community with social and political responsibility. In no way is the Christian ethic left to be a private ethic. As evangelicals we are called to be concerned about such social matters as abortion, pornography, and alcohol and drugs. We should also be concerned about issues such as injustice, exploitation, racism, violence, and the rest. In Romans 13, as John R. W. Stott pointed out at the Pasadena Conference, the apostle Paul stresses the state's authority, its right to arrest, to judge, and to punish, but he also emphasizes that its power is to be used with discrimination.

This subject of the state's use of power suggests what has been called the doctrine of minimal force. The state is responsible for identifying persons who have done wrong and who need to be brought to judgment. Some evildoers are aggressors who threaten the state from outside and thus need to be confronted by the power of the state. Even so, I do not see this clarification of the role of the state as one in which the state has priority in the Christian's life over the Christian's call to live by an ethic of love.

The principles just given, of the Christian's positive relation to the state, are not to be held as absolutes, for it may be necessary to disobey the state if the state should abandon its proper role of punishing the evil and supporting the good and begin supporting the evil and punishing the good. For instance, because of the change of political power in Ethiopia, some of our pastors are in prison for committing themselves first to Christianity. In such cases, believers must resist the state in order to obey God. One should recognize in Romans 13 that the powers that be are ordained by God, which means that God is still above the powers. The Christian's guide for behavior comes not from the social and political orders, but rather from the principles of the kingdom of Christ. Evangelical theologian Carl F. H. Henry, reminding us that there are times in which, with the apostles, "we ought to obey God rather than man," calls us to "efforts to tilt the balance of civil authority from the beast-state (Revelation 13) toward that of the God-state (Romans 13), . . . and let it be known who is the Lord of History and the King of Kings."[3]

Jesus said, "Seek first his kingdom and his righteousness" (Matt. 6:33). In Zechariah 8, we read this word from the Lord: "'These are the things you are to do: Speak the truth to each other, and render true and sound judgment in your courts; do not plot evil against your neighbor, and do not love to swear falsely. I hate all this,' declares the Lord" (vv. 16, 17). And in Zechariah 9:10, the promise of the coming Messiah is that "he will proclaim peace to the nations."

The New Testament adds its many references   123

to the nature of the kingdom, including the statement in I Thessalonians 2:12, that we should "live lives worthy of God, who calls you [us] into his kingdom and glory." And Jesus gives the most penetrating principle of all: "So in everything, do to others what you would have them do to you" (Matt. 7:12). Finally, in I John 4, the Apostle of Love writes, "Dear friends, let us love one another, for love comes from God. Everyone who loves has been born of God and knows God. Whoever does not love does not know God, because God is love" (vv. 7, 8).

Love does not result in a lack of conflict: Intimacy and conflict are inseparable, for we grow in our personal lives through conflict. Intimacy is exceedingly difficult, for we need to know "how to fight" for our improvement, how to avoid judgments that assassinate character, how to resolve differences for mutual benefit, and how to emphasize the covenant of love in our differences. Such love enriches life, makes us pleasant to live with, and uses the values that we have found to enrich the lives of others. Love makes us servants rather than aggressors, and frees us from violence and revenge. President Herbert Hoover said, "We can have revenge or we can have peace, but we cannot have both." In the remarkable Nobel address of Aleksandr Solzhenitsyn, we have these words:

> Let us not forget that violence does not exist by itself and cannot do so; it is necessarily interwoven with lies. Violence finds its only refuge in falsehood, falsehood its only support in violence. Any man who has once acclaimed violence as his method must inexorably choose falsehood as his principle.

124 God's love is his redemptive energy, the gracious extension of himself into man's rebel-

lion and hostility. His activity creates a new order, for in the unmerited love of God believers can become a new people, a people of God's own (see I Pet. 2:9-10). Christ's love always reaches out, confronting, correcting, and calling us to be more like him. God's grace "teaches us to say 'No' to ungodliness and worldly passions" (Titus 2:12); it teaches us to do good, to seek justice, to accept reproach. God's love is self-giving, a participation in our problem even to the extent of the cross. Christ gave himself for us (II Cor. 5:19), and now asks his disciples to be his ambassadors, by loving others.

NOTES

1. John Howard Yoder, *If a Violent Person Threatened to Harm a Loved One . . . What Would You Do?* (Scottdale, Pa.: Herald Press, 1983).
2. Max Weber, *The Methodology of the Social Sciences* (Glencoe, Ill.: Free Press, 1949), pp. 26-27.
3. Carl F. H. Henry, *The Christian Mindset in a Secular Society* (Portland, Ore.: Multnomah Press, 1984), p. 128.

SEXUALITY AND WHOLENESS

8 Peace begins in the home. The "shalom" of God has to do with our total well-being, the wholeness of life. For an ethic of peace to be wholistic it is necessary to face meaningfully the matter of human sexual relationships. According to the Genesis account of the creation of humanity, and Paul's writings in I Corinthians 7 and 11, it took both masculinity and femininity to express the wholeness of the *Imago Dei*. Both male and female are created in the image of God. In the Genesis account of creation, we find the basis for our self-image, our role in relationships, and our sphere of fulfillment. In the differences between male and female, we have the immediacy of a call to peace in the human family. The perpetual rivalry in quests for dominance is answered by the Spirit of Christ, which calls for full respect for one another.

From the beginning, God created them male and female, stating that woman was a helpmeet for man, that is, of the same worth and equal in quality with man. There is no law of creation that makes women in general subordinate to men in general. There is no such thing as a second-class member of the human family. We do not need to give dignity to one another, for God has already given us that dignity in the order of creation; we need to affirm the dignity of one another. The spirit of peace is a surrender of the self's drive for dominance.

True, in what Christian doctrine calls "the Fall," there were consequences that affected   127 relationships, and humans in their sinfulness have perpetuated a relationship by which, in most cultures of the world, woman is subordinated to man. In Jesus Christ, however, all that Adam lost in the Fall has been corrected and restored. Our ideal is not found in the curse but in redemption, in the restoring of full humanness as God intended in creation. In fact, we as believers have more in Christ than Adam and Eve had in their immaturity. According to the Genesis account, Adam and Eve were created innocent, but innocence is not maturity, for maturity comes in the process of making decisions. Adam and Eve made their decisions incorrectly; in contrast, the last Adam, Jesus, made his decisions unerringly; he followed the will of God. Now, through the redemption of Jesus Christ, we as Christians are restored to the wholeness that makes us, in the words of Peter, "as being heirs together of the grace of life" (I Pet. 3:7 KJV). Peace begins at home: Harmony in love is evidence of the open spirit of reconciling love.

In Paul's words, "There is neither . . . male nor female, for you are all one in Christ Jesus" (Gal. 3:28). In Ephesians 5:21, the apostle Paul calls us to submit ourselves to one another in the fear of God. In I Corinthians 11, a unique passage on this relationship, Paul makes clear that the masculine is not complete without the feminine, nor is the feminine without the masculine (see v. 11). He also spells out the relationship between the two sexes from a theological standpoint. The beginning verses of I Corinthians 11 make clear that as God and Christ relate, so man and woman are to relate. This is not to be interpreted as a "chain of command," but is to say that just as God and Christ relate, without meaning that Christ is inferior to God, so man and woman are to relate, without meaning that woman is inferior to man. Jesus makes peace by creating "oneness," a harmony in which each regards the other as created in the image of God equally.

An understanding of sexuality calls for an understanding of the total personality. We should distinguish here between sexuality and sex. Our society is infatuated with sex, and especially with the achievement of sexual orgasm. This emphasis reduces sex to its simplest meaning, rather than seeing it wholistically as the total union of two persons giving themselves to one another in covenant for life. Marriage is intended to be a covenant in fidelity between two persons so that they can know one another in a wholistic, in-depth manner, as will be discussed later in this chapter.

But before addressing further the matter of sex, we need to understand sexuality. This understanding will help us to be enriched in our social relationships and free us from selfishly using another for an experience of sex. By sexuality I mean those various creative, enriching attributes of masculine and feminine personhood that complement humanness. Appreciating sexuality means that the meanings of masculinity and femininity are shared consciously as well as subconsciously in relationships, which are enriched as a result. Peace offers greater rewards to the "love game" than are ever to be found in "macho" expressions.

It is important to focus our attention first of all on adult singleness, an experience that should be the privilege of everyone, and one that is a long-term option for some. Jesus chose singleness, and he enjoyed sexuality without needing sex. This is evident in the account by Luke that there were numerous women in the company of disciples that followed Jesus (Luke 8:1-3). The apostle Paul also chose singleness and argued for it as a good life-style for the   129 itineracy that characterized his evangelistic work (I Cor. 7). Yet he had women as partners in his ministry (see Rom. 16; Phil. 4).

As stated above, singleness is an important experience in the life of the young adult. In fact, it may be said that Jesus opposed marriage for psychologically unweaned persons when he said that one should "leave his father and mother and be united to his wife, and the two will become one flesh" (Matt. 19:5). People need first to find out how to enjoy solitude before they are ready to become partners in marriage. Persons who are not able to be alone are seldom able to endure intense union with other persons. Insecure teenagers too often flee into marriage to hide their confusion or to find a substitute parent. I believe it is necessary that the church teach more clearly that singleness should be enjoyed before marriage is considered. With such an emphasis, the church should devise meaningful ministries for singles. And the reconciling community is where a single person, by associating with persons of both sexes in groups, should be enriched and find identification.

But singleness is also a long-term option for some. The community of faith should not allow people to conclude that marriage is the highest ideal for everyone. The congregation of believers should become an extended family for every member, in which the benefits of sexuality are shared so that masculinity and femininity can enrich the whole congregation, the single and the married. The way of peace refuses to force marriage on one called to be single. In turn, singles can help everyone to remember to put God's work first in life. That is, singles can help those who are married to see that they are to respect Paul's appeal to live "as if not supremely given to marriage" (paraphrase of I Cor. 7:29). Furthermore, since so much of our

130

socializing is ordered around couples and the marriage experience, the church must find ways to incorporate singles in the total life of the family of faith. Singleness is biblical and this fact should be shared by the church in the varied cultural settings in which it exists. A community of the reconciled extends "the peace of acceptance" to each person alike.

In affirming the relation of the masculine and the feminine to each other and the enrichment that they bring to sexuality as a whole, I am not suggesting approval of sexual practices outside the covenant commitment of marriage. Biblical teaching makes clear that a sexual relationship is to be within the covenant of a life commitment. To do otherwise would make of sex simply a hunger that is satisfied by using another person. Throughout the Old Testament, sex properly experienced was always associated with "knowing" another person, and the focus was on the in-depth nature of this relationship. To consider sex an experience not requiring the covenant commitment is to pervert not only the purpose of sex but also the deeper meanings of personhood. For sex to have its intended meaning there must be a relationship between two persons where the covenant and knowing one another deeply are primary.

Another ethical issue related to sexuality concerns the practice of homosexuality. Much attention is given in current writings to physiological and genetic factors that sometimes contribute to homosexuality. Recent studies suggest that the practice of homosexuality is often the expression of an unfulfilled childhood relationship with the parent of the same sex.[1] But others, in their theological reflection, have suggested that some persons were created by God with a homosexual tendency! They regard homosex-   131 uality as a "gift of God" for such persons. In turn, they have then attempted to endorse homosexual marriage as a covenant between persons so conditioned. They regard the covenant of faithfulness between the homosexual partners as the qualification necessary to deem such a marriage acceptable.

It is my conviction that this latter view is both a clear compromise of the biblical position and a compromise of personhood. Those individuals with homosexual tendencies can be accepted in the fellowship of faith, but not in support of homosexual practice. The community of faith should help them to live celibate lives, just as singles who are heterosexual are to live celibate lives. This acceptance and encouragement is possible where fellowship is centered in Christ and does not have as a bottom line the experience of sex with another person.

Even so, for the homosexual to achieve wholeness it is important to look at another aspect of this issue. God created us male and female, and neither the masculine nor the feminine in our sinful state personifies the totality of personhood that should reflect the *Imago Dei*. At its deepest, the covenant of marriage is designed to bring together masculinity and femininity in a way that continually testifies to the transcendence of self, so that two persons can find in this covenant union true peace in the larger meaning of the *Imago Dei*. Homosexuality appears to be a retreat from the demands of this complementary relationship.

It may be that fears arose in the early years of a person's life that altered his or her ability to relate to one who is sexually opposite. This would mean that the homosexual experience is an attempt to find fulfillment in sameness, in the same "understood" gender. To do so allows one to avoid opening up to

132

share with another person who, being different, would enable the other to develop a greater maturity through understandings that emerge in the complementary roles of heterosexual relationships. This would mean that homosexuality is basically a psychological or spiritual rather than a physical issue. The primary question regarding homosexuality has nothing to do with a "Victorian morality" as to how one achieves sexual orgasm, but is rather at root the larger issue of a self-orientation askew. It is my conclusion, then, that homosexuals desire a relationship with persons of the same sex who can more easily be understood and even "controlled."

Having looked at the place of singleness, we turn now to the place and privilege of matrimony. Marriage is God's gift to persons for the enriching and enlarging of their lives on earth together. It is a structure for sharing and for preparing the next generation for its role of life and fulfillment. The marriage covenant is regarded in Scripture as so significant and serious that it is to be a covenant for life. Its seriousness is also reflected in the scriptural injunction that a man is to leave his father and mother and be joined to his wife, and they then become one flesh. That is to say, the man leaves the family of his father and begins a new family unit. His primary loyalty is now to his wife, to whom he gives himself fully. In a similar way, the woman gives herself to her husband with the fidelity that guards her in her friendships. In this way, intimate relationships for both are reserved for the joy of sharing with the spouse.

The ethical aspect of marriage is basically found in the meaning of covenant, that is, the moral ability to make binding commitments by which life will be ordered. In marriage, two persons work out together the deepest meanings of their covenant commit- 133 ments and how they will apply those commitments in all of life's relationships. It is on this particular point that marriages encounter their most severe stress, usually in the second to fourth years of marriage, when the partners move beyond the early stages of their romantic love to face realistically the meaning of covenant. One of the highest moral aspects of the marriage relationship is to discover what it means to be committed "till death do us part," and share a covenant with one person and family. An ethic of peace is demonstrated by two persons in a covenant of mutual esteem. It is "willing" to continue loving; it is cultivating love, "making love" in the largest sense possible.

The increase of the divorce rate, and the attitude that a person can try a marriage and if it doesn't work out satisfactorily try another, are evidence that the meaning of covenant has diminished in our society. Some years ago, president of Harvard Nathan Pusey said, "Men don't want to commit themselves any more; the day of the 100 percenter is gone." Although he was not speaking primarily of marriage, he expressed a characteristic of our times. As a consequence, many persons have the attitude that, rather than enter into a marriage covenant, they should have "open" relationships so that they are "free," rather than committed. By so doing, they reduce the marriage covenant to a marriage contract. This attitude is an expression of fear of what it means to commit oneself to a covenant that is the ground of love. A covenant relationship enables persons to mature together in the experience of life.

The seriousness of divorce lies in the breaking of this covenant. The word *adultery* should be interpreted as covenant breaking, or marriage breaking. We as Christians have too often emphasized the immorality of an experience of sex by a spouse

134

with a third person as adultery, and have not emphasized the adultery as a violation of the covenant, as sin against the other spouse.[2] Fidelity to covenant is the safeguard for a marriage, and it is the key to avoiding adultery in either thought or act. In the frequent adjustments, even tensions, required in a marriage, it is the peace of Christ that binds us together and makes the marriage strong.

Ingredients of a successful marriage include a common faith, continual cultivation of love, creative friendship, and continual respect in family relations. Underlying all of these is the deep meaning of the covenant and an ability to abide by commitments. Gibson Winter, in his book *Love and Conflict*, states that "the average American male is incapable of a happy marriage relationship because he is too selfish to relate intimately to another."[3]

The ability to share ourselves meaningfully with someone else depends largely on our ability to live in honest and open trust with each other. Mutual accountability to covenant makes possible the freedom between spouses that is necessary for them to be liberated in their love. Persons need the intimacy of love in their relationships, but they also need the distance that allows each person to be his or her own self. Such distance is meaningful only where there is implicit trust, and where it is not overextended (see I Cor. 7:5).

The dimensions of faith that determine much of the happiness in Christian marriage are centered in Jesus Christ. It is this common faith that enables the two to become one. In every other area of life, each personality has its differences, but in common faith the two persons meet as one in their relationship to Jesus Christ. A successful marriage is not simply two persons deeply in love with each other, but two persons   135 whose love meets at the common ground of faith in Christ. God creates a "peace of trust" that is exercised by each toward the other. Where there are two there is always the third, the divine presence. This enables a couple to recognize also that even when they are apart, there is always another with them, namely, the person of Christ. This dynamic faith will enable each of the spouses to handle many difficulties and temptations without needing to doubt where they are in relation to the other spouse.

An emphasis on the cultivation of "reconciling love" is a recognition that we do not take one another for granted in marriage. Love needs to be cultivated because of the self-orientation instinct in each of us. Love means that one's life is intimately open to another, and this openness is an act of the will as well as an expression of the emotions. Love is to be cultivated also because of its multi-faceted dimensions. For example, there are three different words that the New Testament uses for love, which are three aspects of the love relationship. These words are *eros*, or erotic love, *phileo*, or friendship love, and *agape*, or enriching love. In marriage all three of these loves are to be enjoyed.

Eros love, for its greatest fulfillment, cannot be pursued apart from the other dimensions of love, or it will leave a person's life empty, having reduced a relationship to primarily emotional and physical passions. However, this eros, or erotic love, is greatly enjoyed between two persons who share a wholistic commitment. Their sexual relationship expresses all the aspects of their personalities.

Second, *phileo*, or friendship love, is to be mutually cultivated, for two persons living in intimate covenant relationship need to develop the satisfactions of friendship, the delight in being together. This

136

means taking time to do things together, learning to share, and also learning to respect the times when one spouse may have some interests that the mate does not fully enjoy. In the Song of Songs we read, "This is my lover, this my friend," (5:16). Friendship is one of the aspects of a marriage that brings a special tone of joy and enrichment into the whole family.

Finally, the enriching love of *agape* is the quality of love that delights in what is brought to the other. Agape love inspires one to think more about serving and enhancing the well-being of the other than of what one is receiving for oneself. It is the ethical aspects of love that provide motivation for the "rightness" of fidelity, honesty, and justice. These, when modeled in the home, are a witness in society of the believer's commitment to the quality of the new life in Christ.

As mentioned above, creative friendship is a necessary ingredient in lasting marriage relationships. My parents celebrated their sixty-eighth wedding anniversary in August 1986. One of the joys we have had as a family has been to watch them make adjustments and changes through the years, and grow in their delight of doing things together. Their respect for each other's hobbies and interests has been a continuing expression of that commitment. In the same way, none of us remains the same person he or she was when first married. As we grow together in marriage, we make changes together. It is important that we express those creative capabilities to continually enrich our friendship and find new things to enjoy doing with each other.

That we do not remain the same person is an advantage in our continuing relationships. Recently, at a general assembly of our denomination, two friends of mine who are identical twins and who roomed with me in the same dormitory during college   137 days, paid my wife a special compliment in their own unique way. The two men approached her during a social time between sessions, and in their typical humorous style, said "Esther, tell your husband that the woman he's living with now is much more attractive than the one he married!" This comment made her day. I in turn enjoyed the compliment as well, for one of the delights of our marriage is the way in which our friendship and respect for each other has continued to grow through the years. In our thirty-six years of marriage, my wife and I have found that growing together is at times costly and painful, for it involves confrontation and change, but also has its benefits, one of the greatest being our association of love. We have greater peace and harmony as our love becomes continually more mature.

To speak of sexuality and wholeness in family life involves confronting parents about their ethical responsibility of teaching all members of the family to understand sexuality with correctness as they grow and mature. This means that children should grow up in an environment where they are loved and where they experience the demonstrations of love. As the perceptive author Charles Shedd has said, "The greatest gift I can give my son is to love his mother." Parents have an ethical responsibility to pass on to their children the right image of what it means to be in love. They should express their affection for each other openly but with good taste before the children, and should speak frankly and reverently of sex and its meaning in relationships. Parents are to cultivate in each child a wholesome attitude toward future involvement in a marriage where love and the sexual experience will fulfill them most, and they should provide an understanding of the place of sex and how it is intended to be enjoyed without guilt or shame. The family is where all members practice enriching one another, confronting one another, and enabling one another as part of a community of love. An adult's happiness in marriage is largely conditioned by the covenant of love in which he or she participated as a developing child.

A successful marriage depends largely on what we bring to the other person. Before marriage, individuals are obsessed with finding the right person. But as soon as one is married, the question changes to that of *being* the right person. There is an ethical responsibility in marriage for each spouse to bring to the other the best possible person for the enrichment of their relationship. The husband should seek to be the best husband, lover, and father that it is possible for him to be. In turn, the wife should seek to be the best wife, lover, and mother it is possible for her to be. Thus, both partners have an ethical responsibility for continuing to grow and to seek the enrichment of their lives. This is to be done individually as well as in those opportunities where the couple expose themselves together in enriching experiences. Such experiences include, among many things, their work and social pleasures, and their sharing together in the life of the church. Common experiences in worship are fundamental to the continued spiritual growth and development of individuals. Marriage enrichment seminars are a significant resource for many couples, for sharing together in such concentrated experiences can enhance their communication and understanding of each other. Further, continuing education courses are available in most communities, where these are offered in areas of personality development, interpersonal relations, resolution of conflict, and other topics. Sessions with qualified counselors, designed to enrich a   139 couple, should not be looked at as something to turn to only in the event of unresolved problems, but can be pursued in a positive way by the couple to aid the growth of their lives together.

My brother David Augsburger has written a number of books that relate especially to developing better communication in marriage. Among them are *The Love Fight, Caring Enough to Confront,* and *Caring Enough to Forgive.* The titles of these books alone suggest dimensions of the marriage relationship in which we must continually maintain an openness to each other and to the growth processes in which each spouse continues to make changes. The ethical priority should be to work at marriage together, complementing each other and encouraging each other in growth.

One of the hazards in today's society is that when both spouses are involved in a professional role, they face the problems of suddenly finding themselves spending most of their time in different worlds. As those worlds become quite important to each spouse, their common world together and their time together may be given less importance. Yet their covenant calls them to the ethical responsibility of placing higher priority on their time together, and planning time together in meaningful and mutually satisfying ways.

Since being in Washington, my wife, Esther, and I have been enriched by the lives of many new friends. Among them are Bill and Dee Brehm, a delightful middle-aged couple whose sparkle and joy in each other is a stimulus to all other couples with whom they associate. On one occasion in a fellowship group, they shared with us a key to this vitality in their love. They related that from the day they were married, they agreed to set apart one evening a week to be their own 140 special evening. On that evening, Bill would come home from work and ceremoniously place his briefcase in the closet and close the door as a sign that he had now left his work for their time together. In turn, Dee would be beautifully dressed for the evening for a special dinner of their own. On occasion, the dinner would be by candlelight at home, at other times an evening out, but it was always a regular experience. One of the rules was that they never talked about finances, their work, or any other subjects with potential to distract them from their joy in each other. Even after the children came into the home, Bill and Dee continued this pattern. This involved their providing dinner for the children and then having their meal together later, often in their bedroom where just the two of them spent the whole evening alone. This weekly "date" communicated to the children that dad and mom considered their evening of friendship and love together important. This pattern has continued through the years and has enriched Bill and Dee's marriage.

The example above emphasizes that persons who take their marriage covenant seriously can find creative ways to continue enriching their marriage and their own personal lives. Both spouses will be stronger, and more free and joyful, in their relations with other persons in society because they are enjoying the in-depth aspects of covenant love.

Notes

1. Elizabeth R. Moberly, *Homosexuality: A New Christian Ethic* (Cambridge: James Clarke and Co., 1983).
2. Lewis B. Smedes, in *Mere Morality*, deals with the nature of adultery as the breaking of covenant (Grand Rapids: Wm. B. Eerdmans Pub. Co., 1983), pp. 165, 180.
3. Gibson Winter, *Love and Conflict* (New York: Doubleday and Co., 1958), pp. 99-100.

DISCIPLESHIP AND THE ENTREPRENEUR

9 An ethic of peace has a lot to do with economics, because on the positive side, human well-being as people and families, and on the negative side, much of the violence in society, are directly related to economic matters. God, in the creation account, calls us to "have dominion" over the created order. We are enjoined to responsible management in both the Old and New Testaments. Above all, we are introduced to the role of stewardship, of managing things that are entrusted to us by God. A major problem in our present social order is how to distribute goods to meet the needs of all persons. There are hundreds of passages in the Old Testament in which the people of God are enjoined to care for the poor, passages implying economic success and management as well as sharing. And there are numerous rules, including Sabbath regulations and the year of Jubilee, to safeguard the freedoms of the poor and the dispossessed.

In the description of the New Testament church found in the book of Acts, one of the unique characteristics of the church that is expressed is the way in which this new community ministered to the needy. It appears that those who had the means were patrons of those who were not so financially blessed. In two passages dealing with the early stages of this new

This chapter was the basis of a lecture at Fuller Theological Seminary in the Payton Lectures, February, 1985.

community, we are told that they "had everything in common," and there were "no needy persons among them" (Acts 2:41-47 and Acts 4:31-35).

If we in the church today would be a people of peace, we must rediscover the New Testament patterns of mutual aid, sharing with those who have need, and thereby enabling them to more effectively serve Christ. There is no easy answer, no quick fix. It is not my opinion that this new community, this new order, is expressed in socialism better than in capitalism. We must seek to discover how that stewardship in community can work. In 1942 the Committee for Constitutional Government at New York released ten guidelines for social and political concerns, which may help those of us who desire to be entrepreneurs. (These guidelines have been attributed to Abraham Lincoln, but according to the Library of Congress, incorrectly.)

1. You cannot bring about prosperity by discouraging thrift.

2. You cannot help small men by tearing down big men.

3. You cannot strengthen the weak by weakening the strong.

4. You cannot lift the wage earner by pulling down the wage payer.

5. You cannot help the poor man by destroying the rich.

6. You cannot keep out of trouble by spending more than your income.

7. You cannot further brotherhood of man by inciting class hatred.

144

8. You cannot establish security on borrowed money.

9. You cannot build character and courage by taking away man's initiative and independence.

10. You cannot help men permanently by doing for them what they could and should do for themselves.

Every society must produce the goods needed for the physical well-being of its members, and make them available justly and equally. Entrepreneurs are persons who take the risks of forming enterprises that will produce the goods a society needs. They take the risks of failure and of loss deciding how to use resources, capital, and labor to market materials that they hope will serve society. The entrepreneur takes a risk by anticipating that by good management there will be profit. It is often at this juncture, the use of profit, that our interest in caring for others more than for our own status is fully tested.

Before we can understand the right management of mammon, we must recognize what is the mismanagement of mammon. Avarice, which is an excessive desire for wealth, can also be thought of as the mismanagement of mammon. Avarice is a common sin against peace. Paul writes that "the love of money is a root of all kinds of evil" (I Tim. 6:10). The love of possessing things has led many people to an obsession with owning things, rather than enjoying them. We in America especially have come to venerate the Bitch Goddess Success. As author and frequent contributor to the *Washington Post*, Henry Fairlie writes that there is "a world wide enterprise of entrepreneurs, to   145 persuade us to buy more than we need and to buy it more expensively than can be morally justified."[1] When we are rich and slaves to a middle-class way of life, we are no longer in charge of our lives; possessions have taken over. We then have neither interest in nor energy for others, and we do not relate with care to our neighbors in society. The recent extreme famine in Ethiopia, for example, is not to be interpreted as a divine act, but is the consequence of decisions made by people of the past, under whose leadership the trees were cut and the land misused with no concern for future generations.

"One of the consequences of avarice," Fairlie says, "that is most strongly condemned in theology is hardness of heart toward the poor, whether in not giving alms to those in need or harshly exacting payment of debts."[2] In 1972, the Canadian Catholic Conference of Bishops issued a proclamation stating, "The riches of Canada are unequally shared. This inequality, which keeps so many people poor, is a social sin." As affluent Americans, we too are guilty of tolerating avoidable poverty when we do not design work and education so that persons can achieve, and instead permit technology to displace them without reassigning them. Avarice cuts people off from other people, and measuring success by how much we possess, we fail to love our neighbor or preserve the land. Our consciences cease to speak to us, and the gap between the "haves" and the "have-nots" continues to increase. Our self-love makes objects of everything and everyone. A significant article in the April 19, 1985, issue of *Christianity Today*, written by Paul Brand, reveals how Emperor Haile Selassie misused the people and the resources of Ethiopia to further enrich the affluent Amharas.

146

To avoid avarice, Jesus taught, we must manage mammon—otherwise mammon will manage us. Christ calls us as believers to a life of responsible freedom in our use of the material, and in a manner that is free from greed. This is only possible when we accept the reign of the sovereign God in our lives. Only when we recognize that God is the owner, and we are simply managers or stewards of the resources that God entrusts to us, can we manage mammon. Jesus said, "No one can serve two masters . . . " (Matt. 6:24).

The apostle Paul in Ephesians 4 instructs us that the Christian "must work, doing something useful with his own hands, that he may have something to share with those in need" (Eph. 4:28). This passage calls us to recognize the privilege and the gift of work. In contrast to a secularity in which one's success is the measure of all things, this passage sets forth a Christian humanness in which the will of God is primary, and in keeping with it we are to behave so as to promote the well-being of all people. This is a theism that regards God as the ultimate, and humanity as next in importance. Such a viewpoint recognizes that all persons are equally of the highest worth because we are all alike made in the image of God. This is fundamental to the pursuit of justice and peace in society.

Applying economic principles that reflect Christ's lordship is especially important in our day. We are living in what has been called a "global village." We are wrestling with the problems of expanding population and the increasing difficulties of adequately allocating both resources and opportunities for work. The problem of the gap between the haves and the have-nots will not go away, but will in fact increase in the next period of history. It is estimated that by the year 2000 there will be some six billion persons in   147 the world; 85 percent of those persons will live in urban settings, and half of these will live in slums.

There is also the problem of technology displacing persons, creating an increase in unemployment. There are the continuing problems that result whenever we elevate the importance of profits over persons. This imbalance is alleviated in some situations by profit-sharing programs. In other situations, there are violations of human rights because there is more concern about the gross national product than about benefits to people. This problem also appears in our churches, where our piety often emphasizes an individualistic relation of salvation and fails to take seriously the whole Jesus and his teachings on the order of the common life. And other problems are inherent in pursuing changes that attempt to correct the inequities found in the systems most prominent in our global village: capitalism and Marxism. A related problem is one of political policies that at times have made governments the guardians of a cruelly unjust status quo in settings where political interests appear to be more important than human rights and the concerns for justice of the populace.

The global village mentality has made us increasingly aware that the resources available are finite. The slices of the pie are getting smaller and smaller, and different groups are each fighting for their piece. The measurements of economic growth need to be adjusted so that we think more of how well we are meeting the needs of the human family than of how much economic security we have acquired. Such principles as justice and equity should guide corporations and individuals in selecting investments and occupations.

One of the sad facts of our day is that the world spends $750 billion annually for military armaments while millions of persons are starving. The evident contradiction here is that the military armaments are justified to defend what we have against other persons who are in need. Human problems could better be corrected if the superpowers would concentrate on the needs of the powerless. The way of peace is first of all the way of love, of caring.

In April 1953, President Dwight D. Eisenhower spoke to the American Society of Newspaper Editors. His statement brings this issue into focus:

> Every gun that is made, every warship launched, every rocket fired signifies—in a final sense—a theft from those who hunger and are not fed, those who are cold and are not clothed. This world in arms is not spending money alone. It is spending the sweat of its laborers, the genius of its scientists, the homes of the children . . . .This is not a way of life at all . . . it is humanity hanging on a cross of iron.

Even in our day, in the face of such far-reaching economic dilemmas, we must recognize that there are theological guidelines for economic pursuits. First, it is important from a biblical perspective that Christians recognize the proper place of business in our society. Too often young evangelicals tend to distrust business because many evangelicals have failed to adequately apply Christian ethics as a corrective to the selfishness that can become a dominant influence in business and professional life. Notwithstanding, it is improper for the new generation to look up to the professions and look down on business. Having worked in educational administration for fifteen years, I must confess that the issues of status and salary are every bit as important to those persons in the professions as they are to persons in business.   149

We need to recognize that business is ordained of God, for we are put in charge of God's resources and told to have dominion over the earth (Gen. 1:28). Business is needed to produce and distribute goods. As the population has increased, the responsibility for the production and distribution of goods has also increased. The developments in our civilization enable us to specialize in various roles, and this is true in business just as it is true in the professions. Business is simply a way to manage resources and to meet human need.

Further, there is a business dimension to almost every human transaction. Although Christian ethics makes service a dominant motive in our relationships with others, we still need to deal effectively with the issue of how we carry out this service. In our personal and family lives it is important that we understand business for stewardship even in making our simple, week-by-week transactions. Christian people need to take seriously both the current management of their resources, as well as management for the future. Developing a budget and drafting a will are significant expressions of stewardship, and of managing wisely the resources that God has entrusted to us.

We must recognize several economic considerations in applying Christian ethics. The first consideration involves basic theories for equally distributing goods and services, for producing these goods and services efficiently, for liberty and freedom for the individual in business, and for conserving resources. In this regard, we are called to consider the global community, the particular problems of the Third World, as well as the ghetto situations in our own society, where people do not have the freedoms even to meet day-to-day family needs.

150

The second consideration has to do with the relation of industry to society. The Christian community must give ethical consideration to the role of a given business, whether it is actually contributing constructively to society. The problems of pollution and the resulting infringements on the well-being of society for the sake of a given business come under ethical judgment. On the positive side, the contributions of industry to the arts and to education make possible the enrichment of society beyond what a given individual might do in simply working for the daily needs of his family. And of course, this consideration has to do with the question of what products ought to be produced, and concerns the principles that guide the producing of goods. This involves considering not only such questions as the growing of tobacco and the size automobile that should be built, but also the production of nuclear armaments, products for chemical warfare, and so forth.

The third economic consideration has to do with managerial ethics. Here we are concerned about such things as equal opportunity in employment practices and transcending discrimination against race or sex. Principles guiding the development of the abilities of employees, promotion, job security, and benefits for the well-being of the employees' families are all a part of Christian ethics in business. Related to these are principles that guide hiring and firing practices so that transitions may be made for the well-being of the person and for the proper allocation of human resources. We should seek to enhance the well-being of persons in their work, and this is possible when we try to see each person as someone with special significance. A further consideration has to do with the proper amount of financial remuneration for work, and the recognition that profits should be made   151 through careful business management and not through improper treatment of employees. Economist Lou Hodges says that a proper expectation is that "people pay for what they get; people get that for which they have paid, and people ought to be able to buy that which they need."

We have moved in history from the family unit to the city-state, to the nation-state, and now we are confronted with the global state, or world economy. We have moved from a barter economy, which can be enjoyed in the markets of Third World countries, to a money economy, where persons can watch the rise and fall of the stock market figures without needing to look in the face of persons who negotiate because of need. We are involved in an economy of large corporations that separate ownership of firms from the persons who manage them, and that create a general alienation from work itself. To discover how work is a gift of God and how we are to enjoy work that fills human needs, is one of the challenges of business ethics.

Applying just economic principles to our economic system is part of the management of mammon, but we must do more. A careful evaluation of economic systems is necessary to ensure justice and equity. It is incumbent upon a society to continually evaluate how well the system to which it is committed meets the needs of its human constituency. If I may paraphrase Jesus, systems are created for humanity, not humanity for systems. There are tremendous strengths in our free enterprise system—it encourages the initiative of the individual, provides the liberty and freedom for persons to carry out their own business interests, and makes efficient production of goods and services possible. I personally favor the present system. But there are also problems in our system, and if it

152

ceases to exist, this will be owing more to human selfishness than to the inadequacy of one of the greater economic experiments of history. Of the problems or dangers in our present economic system in the U.S., there are four in particular that should be noted: (1) It tends to promote acquisitiveness; (2) it tends to produce inequalities that challenge the Christian conscience; (3) there is often an irresponsible use of economic power; and (4) it tends to frustrate the sense of Christian vocation in that it subordinates the primary task of an economy, that of meeting human needs.

In an article entitled "Entrepreneurship: A Risk, an Honor, a Challenge," John W. Eby, head of the business department of Eastern Mennonite College, shared five perspectives by which many Christian entrepreneurs operate. First, they place all of life, including work, under the lordship of Jesus Christ. Second, Christian entrepreneurs, like other Christians, treat their work as a stewardship responsibility given by God, and they live with that accountability. Third, they understand that profit is, ultimately, a means to an end rather than an end in itself. Fourth, as successful entrepreneurs make money, they attempt to find life-styles that reflect their being stewards and not "owners," contributing to the church and society. And fifth, their entrepreneurship extends beyond making money to the form of business itself, leading the business community in promoting values that support high ethical standards, environmental responsibility, and broad employee participation in decision making.[3]

An outstanding example of the Christian entrepreneur developing a corporate relationship is Service-Master Industries of Downers Grove, Illinois. Having personally benefited from ServiceMaster seminars, and the spirit and insight of the first   153 president of the company, Ken Hansen, I applaud their goals: to honor God in all that they do, to help people develop, to pursue excellence, and to grow profitably. With these clear goals, the company has indeed grown. ServiceMaster was featured in *Fortune* magazine in 1984 as the most consistently profitable service company in the U.S. for the decade 1974–1983. This quality of faith in practice, of faithful stewardship, can extend peace and justice in our economic structures.

In his book *The Radical Imperative,* John C. Bennett calls for serious work on structural problems in our economic system, and speaks of four reforms possible in our society. They are: (1) Making Medicare available to the whole population; (2) establishing an income maintenance program that would give to all persons a minimum income; (3) changing the tax system to help distribute wealth more equally; and (4) carrying out the implications of the idea that the federal government is to be the employer of last resort. But we must all want to work at these reforms in order to overcome what John Kenneth Galbraith points to as the contrast between our private wealth and our public poverty.

In order to manage mammon under Christ's lordship, each generation needs to discover how to love people and use things, rather than to use people in its love for things. A commitment to an ethic of peace, to the primacy of "shalom," stresses that the well-being of each person cannot be separated from economic considerations.

The idolatry of the material is one of the greater causes of violence and tyranny in our civilization. The words of Christ in Mark 10:17-22 to the rich young ruler are his answer to this idolatry: "Go, sell everything you have and give to the poor, and you will have treasure in heaven. Then come, follow me" (v. 21).

154

We do not conclude from this story that Jesus prohibits involvement in business occupations where these are second to our vocation to be disciples of Jesus Christ. This passage does make clear, however, that any trust in acquired wealth that places the management of those securities ahead of the vocation of discipleship is an idolatry that must be forsaken. These verses also make clear the direct relation between our privilege in having possessions and our responsibility for helping the poor around us. For example, many Christians drive into Washington, D.C., each morning to work, and then drive back out to the suburbs at the end of the day and close their minds to the conditions and needs of the people in the inner city ghettos. Those who have the means should also have the privilege of sharing.

We cannot underplay the words of Jesus, "But woe to you who are rich, for you have already received your comfort" (Luke 6:24). Nevertheless, how do we share without robbing the other of personal dignity? The "rich" can use their management abilities to enable others to work, to manage their incomes, and to save. In the same passage in Luke, Jesus tells us to love our enemies, to love those who we may feel are encroaching on us and on our desires, and to give to the one who asks of us. Further, Jesus said we should not turn away from the one who would borrow from us. God's word comes through John: "If anyone has material possessions and sees his brother in need but has no pity on him, how can the love of God be in him? Dear children, let us not love with words or tongues but with actions and in truth" (I John 3:17, 18).

Another example of how we as believers can help the needy without condescending would be to assemble a security fund at a bank to serve those who need loans but have no security. A congregation   155 could place such funds in a local bank and approve persons for loans from the bank, not from these funds. Those individuals could then meet their payments to the bank, and thereby build their own credit references. Should one who received a loan default, the bank has the community's security; but more important, the needy person is given an opportunity to achieve with dignity. In such ways, the "haves" enable the "have-nots."

The key to handling things by a Christian ethic is a renewed sense of love. This love for others, matched by a sense of stewardship that manages resources for God, will enable us to share. One of Jesus' disciples, Judas Iscariot, was unwilling to share. What a sermon Jesus' encounter with the rich young ruler must have been to Judas! As in the case of Judas, avarice is bondage; it prevents persons from sharing the true blessedness of life, and the wholeness of relationships.

Economic evils are both structural and personal. Even so, we do need to use structures to serve people. Our American government, when at its best, is not only "of the people" and "by the people," but is also "for the people." Change of structure will not of itself remove the problem, for avarice is intensely personal. A deep work of the Spirit of God that brings us into the joys of stewardship is the only way to a freedom that will let us enjoy one another. Stewardship is a way to peace.

On two occasions, once in Chicago and another time in Cairo, Egypt, my wife, Esther, and I have enjoyed the exhibit of Tutankhamen and his treasures. But, as Henry Fairlie points out, in the end we find something ghastly in the exhibit. The gold and alabaster have kept their form and glitter, but the body has decomposed, and the symbols of the status Tutankhamen 156 achieved tell us nothing of the person he was. "When the stone was rolled away, it was the objects and not the man that rose again."[4] But not so with Jesus, the Christ, for "though he was rich, yet for your sakes he became poor, so that you through his poverty might become rich" (II Cor. 8:9). Jesus affirms our worth by fully sharing himself with us in love. He is our peace.

NOTES

1. Henry Fairlie, *The Seven Deadly Sins* (Washington, D.C.: New Republic Books, 1978), p. 137.
2. Ibid., p. 25.
3. Wally Kroeker, ed., *The Marketplace*, quarterly (September 1985).
4. Fairlie, *The Seven Deadly Sins*, p. 152.

DUALISM OF THE CHURCH AND THE WORLD

10 It has been said that only 5 percent of the people think, 10 percent think that they think, and 85 percent would rather die than think. And of the 10 percent who think that they think, they are simply rearranging their prejudices!

In *Fortune* magazine a few years ago, there was an editorial that said, "In days like these what we of the world need is to hear a word from God. We look to the church for that Word, and all we hear is the echo of our own voice." This is a tragic commentary on the irrelevance of much of the church's activity.

This irrelevance has also been illustrated by the tragic account of the prelates of the church on the eve of the revolution in Russia, who were meeting in session to discuss what would be the proper times for them to wear their yellow robes. We today must think carefully about where the church is compromising with the spirit of our age.

The church is a people identified first and foremost with Jesus Christ. All other loyalties are second to the primary loyalty to Christ. Caesar, or the caesar of any age, is not lord, Jesus is Lord. This faith means that the church responds to the will of God in a way that is not known in general society. The difference of response accounts for radically different ethical decisions and behavior.

An ethic of peace is basically an ethic for the church. Those in society not committed to 159 being disciples of Jesus Christ cannot be expected to live by the ethics of Jesus. The only way the world can enter into the meanings of peace is by the degree to which it recognizes the validity of love and nonviolence in the example of the church as the church follows the teaching of Christ.

The New Testament discusses a tension between the church and the world, a tension that makes clear the uniqueness of the church. Jesus, in positive, creative action, planted his church in the world, saying, "On this rock I will build my church, and the gates of Hades will not overcome it" (literally "prevent me") (Matt. 16:18). On the distinction between the church and the world, Jesus said of the disciples, "They are not of the world any more than I am of the world" (John 17:14). And again, Jesus said, "My kingdom is not of this world. If it were, my servants would fight to prevent my arrest by the Jews" (John 18:36). Even so, this separation from the world has not meant a withdrawal from the world but rather a difference of engagement. Jesus described the church as seed thrown into the world (see Matt. 13:24-30, 37-43). And in his final commission to the disciples, Jesus said, "Therefore go and make disciples of all nations" (Matt. 28:19, 20). It is this mission in the world and to the world that keeps the church from losing its essence.

The church has a responsibility to maintain the fine balance between the task of cultural criticism—or critical consciousness—and the task of compassionate evangelistic service. Nonconformity to the world should mean that one is so conformed to the image of Jesus Christ that there is a radical difference between that person and the world. This difference does not begin by one's studying the world's behavior and then 160 doing something different from it, for that would be allowing the world and its patterns to provide the agenda for one's Christian faith. Rather, the Christian is to be so committed to Christ and the kingdom of God that the difference in his life will be seen and understood by the world.

An illustration would be Gandhi, the Hindu leader, who, although a non-Christian, recognized the value of the teachings of Jesus and sought to practice them. It has been said that Gandhi was a non-Christian with a Christian message, which is to be compared with many Christian people, who have a non-Christian message in that they have missed the meaning of Jesus' teaching of love. Jesus said, "By this all men will know that you are my disciples, if you love one another" (John 13:35). And again, "Everyone who loves has been born of God and knows God" (I John 4:7).

Jesus' call to discipleship is a call to walk with him in the world. By recognizing the dualism this creates, I am not referring to the "Two Kingdom" approach of Luther, an approach that permits the socio-political orders of life to determine much of one's life-style. Rather, participating in the kingdom of God means that a person lives in the world with the critical conscious-ness that frees him to live by the will of Christ. We as believers do not excuse ourselves for violating the will of Christ simply because the orders of the state demand it. The true church is to be free in the world, living by the higher vocation of discipleship with Christ.

But *how* is the church to walk with Christ in the world? First, the church exists by the call of Christ; it takes its very life from the Master. The Greek word *ekklesia*, a term for the church, means a gathering of those who are called into the common fellowship of Christ. This calling is an introduction to a new order, a new life. Jesus, as head of the church, is   161 creating his body by the transforming work of the Holy Spirit. Unfortunately, many persons have reduced their idea of the church simply to a religious organization, and have missed the meaning of persons being new creatures in Christ Jesus. Although a denomination's heritage is valuable in being a history by which one can test how the Spirit has been interacting with a particular people, the basic purpose of the church is not to identify ethnically with a heritage.

Paul writes of an essential calling of the church when he says,

> Therefore, I urge you, brothers, in view of God's mercy, to offer your bodies as living sacrifices, holy and pleasing to God—this is your spiritual act of worship. Do not conform any longer to the pattern of this world, but be transformed by the renewing of your mind. Then you will be able to test and approve what God's will is—his good, pleasing and perfect will. (Rom. 12:1, 2)

"Nonconformed" comes from the Greek word *metamorphousthe,* meaning a metamorphosis, a change caused by an inner transformation that permeates the whole of one's being. What is more, Paul uses the phrase "the renewing of your mind" to show that Christianity is a matter of positive understanding of the will of God and of an intelligent response to God's will. If we think of Christianity only as negative and restrictive, we have surrendered the possibilities of creative fulfillment. In contrast, we as disciples of Christ are called to identify positively with the will of God.

The life of the church is the life that is mediated to it by the head of the church, Jesus Christ. And the Good News of the gospel is that we can be children of God; we can share in the privilege of being new creatures in Christ. As Paul writes, "If anyone is in Christ, he is a new creation; the old has gone, the new has come" (II Cor. 5:17). Anglican missionary to India Lesslie Newbigin asks, "Why do people preach everything at us but the gospel? Why use all other sources but the Scripture?" An institutionalized church will inevitably swing to humanitarianism, to things that can be structured and achieved whether its members are praying or not. An intellectualized church will tend to shift to idealism rather than experiencing a relationship in reconciling grace, to an armchair theology that acts as though if its members have discussed an issue, they have done what was needed. An internalized church will become acculturated and ethnic, oriented to the concerns of the in-group, and will lose the cutting edge of the gospel in Christ's mission to society.

The second way in which the church is to walk with Christ in the world is for it to realize that it receives its life-style from Jesus. The Christian faith has its own world view, which is not to be left in generalities, but must become a guide for the ordering of the common life. Christianity is not a mystical, pious retreat from real-life situations. In fact, because it takes the whole of life seriously, former archbishop of Canterbury William Temple has described Christianity as the most materialistic of all religions. One does not retreat from life in an attempt to achieve holiness. Rather, God sanctifies the believer's approach to the whole of life, and that individual can then appropriate the material resources to the praise of God and the well-being of others.

This approach to life calls for some specific and personal applications of Christian faith to 163 life's practice. American theologian Reinhold Niebuhr has said, "There is an increasing tendency for modern men to imagine themselves ethical because they have delegated their vices to larger and larger groups." Too often individuals find it easy to dodge personal responsibility, leaving it to some nameless body or committee. Although committees are important resources for broad counsel, they may become tools through which persons avoid carrying personal responsibilities. My wife, Esther, and I once saw an epitaph on a tombstone in a churchyard in the Cotswold of England that may offer some wise caution on committee work. The inscription read, "He died in committee."

In Romans 14 the apostle Paul calls each of us as believers in Christ to apply our principles to our personal life-styles, saying, "Everything that does not come from faith is sin" (Rom. 14:23). Principles must inevitably be reduced to practice, and the community of believers has a responsibility to one another in interpreting the guidelines for practice. We are not to make individualistic interpretations, but are called to share with the fellowship of believers our search for the mind of the Spirit and its applications. This is the social setting of peacemaking.

This understanding of discipleship involves not only personal habits, but social relationships and occupational identifications as well. In his very prophetic book *The Politics of Jesus*, John Howard Yoder develops the theology of an ethic of discipleship. In chapter 7, entitled "The Disciple of Christ and the Way of Jesus," Yoder shows how the way of Jesus is interpreted in the New Testament epistles, and how the believer's understanding of Jesus today as the ideal of Christian ethics is to be wholistic and not selective.[1]

Our vocation being that of discipleship in

Jesus Christ, we have a responsibility to apply the meanings of this vocation to our respective occupations. When we take the vocation of discipleship seriously, we will be selective in occupational choices. The choice of occupation is to be determined by our primary vocational calling of being disciples of Jesus Christ. Ethical decisions about life-styles are to reflect the consistent application of basic Christian principles to the orders of life. This not only rules out occupations such as prostitution, gambling, and drug trafficking, but for most of us, would also rule out working in fields that relate to chemical warfare, biological warfare, nuclear arms, and so on. And for many of us, discipleship excludes all involvement in warfare itself.

The third way in which the church is to walk with Christ in this world is to express the "love-style" that it receives from Jesus. It is said that love is not simply something you feel, it is something you do. We as members of the new community in Christ are called to practice love, that is, to open our lives deeply and personally to others so that our sharing can be for their good and enrichment. Love is never selfish, it does not manipulate people, it does not take advantage of others, and it refuses to use others for its own ends. The classic expression of love is found in I Corinthians 13. In this chapter Paul lists eight positive aspects of love, and eight negative things that love prevents.

The personification of this love is Jesus. His love knew no limits. He gave himself to the death rather than defend himself. His whole life was one of love; he ministered compassionately to the poor, healed the lame, the dumb, and the blind, and exposed the crippling aspects of prejudices of those who professed to be leaders. Whether Christ's love was expressed in healing or in judgment, it was a 165 ministry for the well-being of humanity. Jesus' love was ultimately expressed in his pledging his life to the death for the redemption of humanity. The love-style he modeled for his disciples was one of self-giving even to the extent of dying on the cross.

Today, the church, Christ's body, is called to live under the cross that he endured. Jesus said, "If anyone would come after me, he must deny himself and take up his cross daily and follow me" (Luke 9:23). The apostle Paul said, "I fill up in my flesh what is still lacking in regard to Christ's afflictions" (Col. 1:24). Again, Paul, writing to Timothy, said, "In fact, everyone who wants to live a godly life in Christ Jesus will be persecuted" (II Tim. 3:12). Just as the Messiah came as a suffering servant rather than as a conquering king, so we as his disciples are called to a suffering role of active love as a triumph of meaning, even in the face of the most repressive acts.

The Anglican archbishop John Janani Luwam was executed in 1977 on false charges brought by the Ugandan dictator, Idi Amin. Although forbidden to conduct a funeral service, and not having the archbishop's body, the church in Uganda gathered around an empty grave to remember Luwam and responded to tyranny by affirming its faith in Christ's resurrection. The church's faith was undaunted in the face of suffering, for the people knew the meaning of Peter's words, "Christ suffered for you, leaving you an example, that you should follow in his steps" (I Pet. 2:21).

We in the church are called by Jesus Christ to walk in his will, to be members of his body, to live as members of the kingdom of God. Commitment to service rather than power marks the true church. Christ's disciples practice mutual aid, and share at a significant cost to themselves for the well-being and development of others. In contrast, the world lives by the rules of selfishness, operates by the drives and instincts of the "herd," and deports itself according to the lusts of the flesh. The world is committed to seeking status and power rather than heeding the call of discipleship. It functions by seeking to safeguard what it has for its own pleasure rather than discovering the meanings of love.

Even though the world has become a global village, it knows little of a global community where even enemies can be treated as brothers. Society continues rather to treat brothers as enemies, dividing the human family into camps bent on destroying one another for the sake of self-preservation. In contrast, the church knows the meaning of a fellowship that transcends national lines and that seeks to unite people around the globe with the awareness of mutual participation in the body of Christ.

In July 1983, my wife, Esther, and I were privileged to participate in the World Congress on Evangelism, held in Amsterdam under the sponsorship of the Billy Graham Evangelistic Association. There were more than 4,000 persons present, representing 135 nations of the world, including almost all of the Eastern European Communist countries. It was a gathering in which the Third World had primary representation, and those of us from the West were an obvious minority. With all of this diversity, there was a remarkable oneness in Christ, a fellowship in the Spirit as we met together in worship and to encourage one another in the work of Christ. The following week, the World Council of Churches began its meeting in Vancouver, British Columbia, witnessing in another ecclesiastical circle to the reality of the global nature of the church of Jesus Christ. The Holy Spirit is teaching us that the key to changing the global community is not to be   167 found in political solutions but in spiritual priorities. Peace involves building a network of faith in Jesus Christ around the globe. His kingdom is eternal, which means that it has already begun.

NOTES

1. John Howard Yoder, *The Politics of Jesus* (Grand Rapids: Wm. B. Eerdmans Pub. Co., 1972), pp. 115-43.

THE KINGDOM OF GOD AND THE POWERS OF THE WORLD

11 God's kingdom is universal, it is transnational, and it offers grace to the whole human race. His reign is expressed in principles of love, justice, peace, and equity, and it motivates his people to serve one another. As we discussed in the previous chapter, this service stands in direct contrast to the kingdoms of the world, which operate by power and violence for the sake of self-preservation. Donald Kraybill, professor of sociology at Elizabethtown College, emphasizes this unique difference in his book *The Upside-Down Kingdom* (see Bibliography).

Jesus came preaching the kingdom of heaven. He did this in a society that was under the dominion of the Roman Empire. He presented the rule of God so clearly that the call to live by God's will was understood by those who heard him. At the same time, he avoided being a zealot or an insurrectionist lest he reduce the message of the kingdom to that of violent opposition to political tyranny. This is expressed by what John Howard Yoder calls "The politics of Jesus," the recognition by Christ of the primacy of the rule of God.[1]

Being a part of the body of Christ, of the people of God, we have freedom amid the various kingdoms of this world. This is the only way in which people can possibly live with sanity in the face of human tyranny.

God's people, who live by the orders of the new life, live by the ethics of love, justice, and 169 peace. But in order to pursue this new life in the world, we must understand our relationship to the social and political forces of this world. The New Testament picture describing the political order is not as singular as many would imply. In the New Testament, the political order is not seen as an extension of the Old Testament civil orders that governed the nation of Israel. Israel existed as a theocracy under the immediate rule of God. The New Testament church is not a civil power, is not a continuation of this Old Testament political Israel. The church is a new people of God, not identified with any nationality, but a global or universal community. And with respect to a view of secular government, the New Testament presents a varied picture. In Romans 13, government is spoken of as a servant of God, and in Revelation 13, governments are described as servants of Satan. The difference depends on whether a government respects God's order or has turned to the idolatry of power.

Throughout Scripture there is abundant evidence that government has its identity as a servant for the well-being of society. It is to recognize the higher law of a sovereign God. It is also clear, however, that power moves persons to idolize that power. National power becomes idolatrous.

According to the apostle Paul in Colossians 2, Jesus "disarmed the powers and authorities" (v. 15). That is, he unmasked the powers; he exposed their true nature so that we as believers would not give our ultimate loyalty to such powers. Reformed theologian Hendrick Berkhof says: "No powers can separate us from God's love in Christ. Unmasked, revealed in their true nature, they have lost their mighty grip on men. The cross has disarmed them: wherever it is preached, the unmasking and the disarming of the Powers

170

takes place."[2] Even so, the Christian is not to be anti-government, for the government is ordained of God to keep order in society; it is designed to protect the innocent and punish the guilty. An ordered society is one in which the government constantly upholds the highest ethical morality professed by its constitution and constituents. A good government is one that secures the freedoms and human rights of all of its people for the well-being of the whole.

Government is primarily secular; being secular, it is to remain neutral on spiritual matters. The First Amendment to the Constitution of the United States holds that "Congress shall make no law respecting an establishment of religion, or prohibiting the free exercise thereof." This amendment provides the freedom for the church to be the church in society. In this sense, a secular government can be a good government, even though a secular church would be a rotten church. While holding to separation of church and state as organizations, the Christian does not separate the sacred from the secular, but influences the secular for cultural enrichment.

A government should be the servant of its people and not a power platform for the elite. There is no end to the list of atrocities perpetrated by persons bent on maintaining or increasing their power. The statement by Lord Acton has been demonstrated in history: "Power tends to corrupt and absolute power corrupts absolutely." Persons who choose the course of violence need to understand that the forms of violence "destroy the soul of the perpetrator as surely as the life and health of the victim."[3] In fact, it is where governments have a benevolent relationship with their subjects that they are the most secure. History demonstrates that the people win; this is to say that eventually, often at   171 great cost, tyranny fails. It is the mission of the church in society to help persons in the political order recognize that preserving human rights is not a program of government, it is the purpose of government.

The judgments in Revelation, chapters 16–19, are judgments on the political, social, and economic structures of the world. The ultimate victory of Christ is shown when, as these political powers (i.e., Babylon) fall, the kingdom of God lives on. The answer that comes from chapter 19 is that the redeemed of the Lord are still able to say "Hallelujah" when the securities of this world vanish.

Our calling as Christians is to support the government in securing human rights and the well-being of all citizens. Christians are not only to be interested in an ordered society, they can contribute to the development of such a society. There are certain rights that should be extended to all peoples. Such rights, most evangelicals hold, should include the right to life, the right to self-determination, the right to land and space, the right to adequate food, the right to be treated with justice, the right to worship in freedom of conscience, the right to a good education, the right of families to teach their children values and faith amid pluralism, and the right to a future unspoiled by ecological perversions. Such rights are for the well-being of all people. The pursuit of such rights is enriched by the ethical perspectives and qualities of the Christian community within society.

The enriching contribution of the church should in no way be an attempt on the part of Christians, through the church, to control government or to make government an extension of the church. Church and government are to remain separate, but they are also to respect a dualism in which each can hold the other accountable for its own basic commit-

172

ments. Movements by Christians to "take over" or "Christianize" the government in a rejection of pluralism violate this principle of separation of church and state. It is, however, part of life and faith that Christian influence will be shared with government, just as all other humanistic influences are shared. Our government in the United States is one "of the people, by the people, and for the people," and we as Christians in this country are a part of these people.

A government of a given nation is to be enriched by, confronted by, and held accountable by the Christian community, which is a part of the citizenship. Christians do not withdraw from responsible interaction with the structures of society. A basic contribution of the Christian community in any given society is to demonstrate the proper use of power by a government as a privilege in its influence on others.

Max Weber, the great German social scientist, defined power as the ability of one person to win the submission of another person to his or her purposes. Christians recognize that only love will protect one's use of power from becoming tyranny. While the ethic of love cannot be expected of the unregenerate persons in society, the Christian community can help the political figures in that society to live according to higher ideals, and to understand that power is exploitative when used to diminish the power of other persons.

The church is not to pit its power against the power of the political order. Instead, the church is called to show how the proper goal should be an equality of meaningful relationships rather than a duel for mastery. Jesus did not call us as his disciples to a negative identity, but to positive action. Christians should be a witness to the government that it exists by the franchise of the people, and that the people are to be heard.   173

Leaders of government are also our neighbors, those whom we profess to love. Love calls us to do something about the ethical vacuum on the issue of violence. At the Mennonite World Conference of 1962, held in Kitchener, Ontario, the late veteran missionary Nelson Litweiler spoke to this concern:

> If we are ever to see a permanent cessation of nuclear tests, if there is ever to be a humane and sane attitude toward other races, if the rich are to share with rather than exploit the poor, if human life will ever be considered sacred in many areas of the world, if life is to be respected, if any steps are to be taken toward sanity in human relationships, it will certainly be because of public opinion being aroused, making statesmen and governments aware of the popular sentiment. And if the church does not awaken the consciences of the people, who will?[4]

While Jesus was not a zealot or a "freedom fighter," he did relate in solidarity with his followers. He spoke with conviction to political leaders in the Jewish Sanhedrin, and spoke frankly of King Herod and of Caesar. Jesus referred to Herod as a fox, and deliberately avoided confrontation with him (see Luke 13:31-35). When Jesus was finally brought into the presence of Herod as a part of his trial, he refused to give Herod any answers that would affirm the power structure by which Herod operated. In his silence Jesus gave evidence that he was not subject to the political schemes of this puppet king. With respect to Caesar, Jesus confounded his critics by saying, "Give to Caesar what is Caesar's, and to God what is God's" (Matt. 22:21). Jesus himself modeled the fact that when you give to God all that is God's, there is little 174   problem over what is left being given to Caesar.

Similarly, throughout the Old Testament there is no hesitancy on the part of the prophets to declare the Word of God to their political leaders. This was true both of prophets confronting the kings of Israel and Judah and of those speaking to the leaders of other nations, such as Pharaoh in Egypt, or Nebuchadnezzar, or Darius the Mede.

The prophetic word from God holds all persons alike accountable before the sovereign Lord. It is a part of the mission of the Christian community to confront society with the evidence that there is a standard of right to which all persons are held accountable, and that this standard is not determined by majority vote. Sociologist and theologian Franklin Littell, of Temple University, has written of how Protestant church leaders condemn themselves when they attempt to use political sanctions to enforce upon all society moral obligations that they cannot through preaching enforce in their own church membership. The Christian community should achieve its goals by convictions of truth, not by the coercion of the state.[5]

In the eighteenth century, the Mennonite community in Pennsylvania, living in early settlements under the leadership of William Penn and his Quaker fellowship, confronted its society with a refusal to own slaves and enter into this inhumanity. John Wollman, himself a Quaker, became convinced that slavery was wrong and so began a reformation, first of his Quaker community and then of the larger society. As a result of the revivals conducted by Charles Finney, there developed a strong conviction for Christian social responsibility. Many abolitionists were abolitionists owing to an experience with Christ in the revival movement. The Christian church was thus used by God to create a consciousness in society of the injustice of slavery. 175

In the twentieth century, Martin Luther King became a voice in the United States for civil rights and turned the nation around. He appealed to the conscience of the nation using Christian principles. At the present time, the voices of many in the Christian community across America and the world are being heard in protest against the nuclear arms build-up, and they are calling on the world powers to agree to a nuclear freeze. But tragically, there are conservative voices in the Christian community who support the power struggle by the use of violence because they are conditioned more by a status quo, nationalistic conservatism than by the principles of the kingdom of Jesus Christ. It is important to explode the myth that if one is conservative in one's theology, it follows that one must also be conservative in political and social views. The truth of the matter is that even though my theology is conservative—I believe in the actual resurrection of Jesus Christ, the authority of Scripture, and the reality of the rule of Christ—I am free to select my political and social views. The Christian should at times be politically conservative and at times more liberal, depending on what he or she believes is the more appropriate expression of the will of Christ on a given issue.

In the Latin American Catholic church, the attempt to confront political powers with a Christian witness has been labeled "Liberation theology." Greater clarity on the part of exponents of Liberation theology regarding the separation of church and state and nonviolent means of working for human rights, could strengthen the impact of a Christian conscience in Latin America in ways that would not lead to violent confrontation between church and state. Theologian and author Brian Hebblethwaite, in his work *Christian Ethics in the Modern Age*, states that Liberation theology has tended to equate redemption and liberation: "It neglects the fact that a man can be redeemed even though he remains politically in bondage and that men can be liberated politically without being redeemed."[6] He further points out that the chief criticism of Liberation theology "has been over its willingness to give moral support to violent revolution or guerrilla warfare, and occasionally to participate in it, for it seems that no other way can be expected to bring about the liberation of the oppressed."[7]

With this criticism we should recognize that Liberation theology has come to the fore in part because of the inadequacy of the Christian church in Latin America to recognize how an evangelical faith can be involved in social concern. But Liberation theology may be a witness to the political power structures, confronting Latin American governments with their need to achieve more evident human rights for the common people.

Despite the myriad differences among societies and governments around the world, Jesus calls his disciples to be peacemakers wherever they are. He fills his disciples with his love, through the agency of the Holy Spirit. The apostle Paul commented on this mission of peacemaking in Romans 12: "As far as it depends on you, live at peace with everyone" (v. 18). When a person knows the transforming grace of Christ and the indwelling power of the Holy Spirit, there is much more that lies within that person than what he or she may have initially recognized.

Christ's followers can find ways for witness in dialogue, for responsible participation to decrease the violence in our global village, and to help nations work for peace when they are at an impasse owing to trying to save face while continuing to run the   177 risk of a global holocaust. We as believers can call on the Christian community of which we are a part to put its priorities on sharing its resources with the 1 billion persons in the world who are suffering from malnutrition, rather than on protecting what we have. We can work with relief agencies to help refugees in their plight. At the end of 1983, there were more than 3 million Afghan, 2 million Palestinian, nearly 1 million Ethiopian, ¼ million Indo-Chinese, ¼ million El Salvadoran, ¼ million Angolan, nearly ¼ million Ugandan and more than 200,000 Burundian, 150,000 Rwandan, and 75,000 Namibian refugees, as reported in *USA Today*.

The Christian community today must seek to demonstrate the biblical meaning of justice. In the Old Testament high-water mark of ethical instruction, Micah says, "He has showed you, O man, what is good. And what does the Lord require of you? To act justly and to love mercy and to walk humbly with your God" (Mic. 6:8). Throughout the Old Testament, God demonstrated an aggressive concern for justice-righteousness. The prophet Amos said, "But let justice roll on like a river, righteousness like a never-failing stream!" (Amos 5:24). The church helps renew society's commitment to work for justice by sharing the Word and its life as a worshiping people. From his pastoral ministry, J. H. Oldham wrote, "There is nothing greater that the church can do for society than to be a center in which small groups of persons are together entering into this experience of renewal and giving each other mutual support in Christian living and action in secular spheres."[8]

For a biblical understanding of justice, one must first recognize that justice originates in God's

178   covenant to deal with humanity in justice. God

deals with people in justice, and they should enter into a covenant with him in order to be able to deal with one another in justice. Justice toward others is an extension into the social order of this covenant with God. Through Jesus Christ, people who were separated by race or nationalism before are brought together into a new community of peace (see Eph. 2:16). This new community models the "shalom" of God and expresses this "shalom" in the justice-righteousness of human relationships.

In the biblical understanding of justice, there are positive dimensions of repentance, correction, and restoration. Justice is not simply paying another back in kind. Justice is rather the correcting and restoring of persons who perpetuate or are caught in injustice. In the third chapter of Romans, the Atonement is expressed as God's way of dealing justly with man to correct man's rebellion and bring humanity back into harmony with himself (see Rom. 3:25-26). From this perspective, justice is not fulfilled simply by punishing the offender, but rather by correcting the underlying problem. In like manner, a just government should also move to correct the problems of injustice for its people.

For example, capital punishment can be thought of as justice only if justice is conceived of as paying back in kind for a wrong committed. But capital punishment does not fulfill the meaning of justice unless in some way it helps correct the problem that has produced the offender. The need for such correction would be better met by having society continually relate to offenders, who would be required to make restitution for their nonviolent crimes. Imprisoning persons for committing violent crimes reminds society of the need to correct the injustices that produce violent criminals.

Justice is not served when the poor are   179

punished for taking from the rich if nothing is being done by the wealthy to provide opportunities for work, educational scholarships, and food for those who feel themselves trapped in systems that leave them feeling hopeless. But while sharing our resources may appear to alleviate the problems of injustice, it may really perpetuate the injustice if done with condescension, or by bringing persons into cultural servitude. Structural injustices may readily cancel out charitable efforts, for structural injustice, which limits opportunity for the poor or non-dominant race, continues to contribute to imbalance in society. The need to protect the rights of minorities; resolve the inequities in wages in some pay scales; establish fair credit policies for those who need help but may be overcharged because they are a greater risk; avoid the practice of red-lining[9] in housing areas, and instead help redevelop those sections; and resist discrimination because of race, all call us as Christ's followers to work for structures that are more just in our society.

An ethic of peace not only tells us as believers what is and what ought to be, but it also motivates us to live in the "shalom" of which we speak. Such a commitment to the "shalom" principle, to the well-being of others, finds its directive in the Master. Jesus said, "The kings of the Gentiles lord it over them; and those who exercise authority over them call themselves Benefactors. But you are not to be like that" (Luke 22:25-26a). In this context Jesus taught that the chief characteristic of discipleship should be that of service. In a secular environment each person considers personal achievement to be a right. The teachings of Jesus sharply contradict this stance. Jesus said, "If anyone wants to be first, he must be the very last, and the servant of all" (Mark 9:35).

When Jesus came announcing the kingdom, the Jewish community had been expecting a Messiah who would lead them by the use of political power to political achievements for their personal and national security. When Jesus began his ministry in solidarity with the needy and the humble, even John the Baptist had to send someone to ask Christ, "Are you the one who was to come, or should we expect someone else?" (Luke 7:20). John the Baptist was asking whether Jesus was indeed the Messiah, because the reality of Jesus' Messianic ministry was radically different from that of the image of the political leader whom the term *Messiah* had always suggested. Jesus' response was to tell John of a ministry that was creating a new community enjoying the "shalom" of God. This Messiah was to be understood as the suffering servant of Isaiah 53 rather than as a conquering king.

If justice is the correction of the problem, then the sharing of the *kerygma*, the Good News of the gospel, is an essential aspect of working for justice. In recognizing that the principles of peace, love, and justice are not fully experienced or expressed apart from the grace of God, we as Christ's disciples recognize that the unregenerate cannot practice the Christian ethic. It is therefore incumbent upon the church to share the gospel of Jesus Christ so that persons who do not know God can experience his transforming grace and thereby bring to their social circle the renewing grace of God in justice, love, and peace. Living out a life based on an ethic of peace is possible only when people enjoy the fellowship of the Prince of Peace.

It is Christ who has liberated us to be a new people of God in the world. He created the church as a totally new community of two types of people, Jew and Gentile, and in so doing, he unmasked the   181

powers that had become pseudo-gods. Hendrik Berkhof, Reformed theologian, said it clearly:

> Thus Christ has "triumphed over them." The
> unmasking is actually already their defeat. Yet this is
> only visible to men when they know God Himself has
> appeared on earth in Christ. Therefore we must think
> of the resurrection as well as of the cross. The
> resurrection manifests what was already accomplished
> in the cross: that in Christ, God has challenged the
> Powers, has penetrated into their territory, and has
> displayed that He is stronger than they.[10]

Our commitment, then, is for the church of Christ to
be his agent in society. As John Howard Yoder says:
"The church does not attack the powers; this Christ has
done. The church concentrates upon not being seduced
by them. By her existence she demonstrates that their
rebellion has been vanquished."[11] We as Christ's
followers are free to obey Christ, free to be conscien-
tious objectors, and free to be a people of peace in a
global community.

NOTES

1. John Howard Yoder, *The Politics of Jesus* (Grand Rapids: Wm. B.
   Eerdmans Pub. Co., 1972), pp. 135-62.
2. Hendrik Berkhof, *Christ and the Powers* (Scottdale, Pa.: Herald Press,
   1962), p. 30.
3. John C. Bennett, *The Radical Imperative* (Philadelphia: Westminster
   Press, 1975), p. 77.
4. Mennonite World Conference at Kitchener, Ontario, *The Lordship of
   Christ* (Scottdale, Pa.: Mennonite Publishing House, 1962), p. 226.
5. Franklin Littell, *From State Church to Pluralism* (New York: Doubleday
   and Co., 1962), p. 120.
6. Brian Hebblethwaite, *Christian Ethics in the Modern Age* (Philadelphia:
   Westminster Press, 1982), p. 93.
7. Ibid., p. 94.
8. Quoted in Yoder, *Politics of Jesus*, p. 155.

9. A term used in inner-city real estate actions, where banks designate an area as unacceptable for aid, and insurance agencies refuse to cover property in a section of the city, permitting it to go to ruin.
10. Berkhof, *Christ and the Powers*, p. 31.
11. Yoder, *Politics of Jesus*, p. 153.

EVANGELISM, A THEOLOGY OF RECONCILIATION

12 Evangelism is the channel through which God meets persons. To be involved in evangelism is to make Jesus available to persons, all persons. Our task as evangelists is to create a theological and cultural environment in which the reconciling love of Christ is shared, for we are agents of God's peace. "We are therefore Christ's ambassadors, as though God were making his appeal through us" (II Cor. 5:20). Rightly understood, evangelism is the ultimate in peacemaking, for it calls persons to reconciliation with God, to confess Jesus as Savior and Lord, to walk with the Prince of Peace. Evangelism is not an appendage to theology, it is an essential aspect of a theology of reconciliation, and reconciliation is the way to peace.

The "peacemaker" seeks to win persons to openness to Christ. The evangelical person can never share in destroying the life of anyone, because Christ died for everyone; rather, that person is out to win them to becoming brothers and sisters in Christ. Jesus came, "not to be ministered unto, but to minister," and so we too are called to minister to others. Jesus said, "As the Father has sent me, I am sending you" (John 20:21). We are sent to be his agents of reconciliation.

We are also called to recognize what God intends this world to be and then to interpret his will for and through

This chapter was the fifth lecture in the Payton Lectures, Fuller Theological Seminary, February 1985.

the church in the world. We become God's voice of reconciliation. As Paul wrote to Timothy: "This is good, and pleases God our Savior, who wants all men to be saved and to come to a knowledge of the truth. For there is one God and one mediator between God and men, the man Christ Jesus, who gave himself as a ransom for all men" (I Tim. 2:3-6).

In his second letter to the Corinthians, Paul expressed the essential theology of evangelism:

> Therefore, if anyone is in Christ, he is a new creation; the old has gone, the new has come! All this is from God, who reconciled us to himself through Christ and gave us the ministry of reconciliation: that God was reconciling the world to himself in Christ, not counting men's sins against them. And he has committed to us the message of reconciliation. We are therefore Christ's ambassadors, as though God were making his appeal through us. We implore you on Christ's behalf: Be reconciled to God. (II Cor. 5:17-20)

God comes to humanity in grace. God takes the initiative. Having done so throughout "salvation history" but ultimately in the Incarnation, God continues to confront us by the presence of the risen Savior in the body of Christ, the church. We who believe, who are disciples of Christ, share the mission of reconciliation. Our God "so loved the world that he gave his one and only Son" (John 3:16). This Son, Son of God and Son of Man, "came to seek and to save what was lost" (Luke 19:10). In turn, God has committed unto us the work and the word of reconciliation (see II Cor. 5:19).

A question frequently asked of me as an evangelist is how to relate a call to peace and nonviolence to
186   evangelism. One answer is that we should

distinguish between the *didache* or teachings, and the *kerygma* or gospel. This distinction may help to identify particular content in preaching, but from my perspective, the unity of the Word of Christ in the ministry of reconciliation does not permit our separating *didache* and *kerygma*. Doctrinal teachings *(didache)* are aspects of our understanding the implications of the reconciling gospel *(kerygma)*. One does not evangelize persons to an ethical system, but to Christ, to a relationship with God. As people are won to Christ by the Good News *(kerygma)* they are won to the Christ-life *(didache)*. This commitment to Christ is a relationship, a direction, not an achievement of perfection. To teach people less than this is to lead them to a partial understanding of Christ.

The church is truly the church of Christ when it is faithful to its evangelistic mission. This mission of evangelism, however, is not to be construed solely as a role. The church is called to be a presence in society as well as a voice. Ecumenical theologian Theodore Wedel has described the Christian mission as presence, service, and communication, and I would add, in that order. My own definition is that evangelism is sharing in everything that makes faith in Christ an option or a possibility for people.

John A. MacKay said, "Evangelism, the confrontation of men with Jesus Christ so that they may accept him as their Savior and follow him as their Lord in the fellowship of the church, is the church's primary task." When this is recognized, it will enable a church to be open to others rather than being a closed circle of ethnic worshipers. It will enhance the ability of the members of a congregation to be enablers of one another, to recognize the various gifts of one another, and to equip one another for serving Christ. Paul 187 wrote that the risen Christ gave gifts to the church "to prepare God's people for works of service" (Eph. 4:12).

As evangelists, we are interpreters of Christ in many and varied cultures. While I hold a high Christology, I am aware that Christology is our interpretation of Christ, and we must interpret Christ from the Scripture as the one authority about Christ, even while doing so in an unfamiliar culture setting. This awareness has led missionary to India Lesslie Newbigin to say:

> Christology is always to be done in via (on the way) at the interface between the gospel and the cultures which it meets on its missionary journey. It is of the essence of the matter that Jesus was not concerned to leave as a fruit of his work a precise verbatim record of everything he said and did, but that he was concerned to create a community which would be bound to him in love and obedience, learn discipleship even in the midst of sin and error, and be his witness among all peoples.[1]

It is this mission of interpreting Jesus under the guidance of the Spirit that enables the proclamation of Christ to be relevant in every culture. But the interpretive task also calls us to be faithful to the uniqueness of the person of Jesus Christ. In expressing the gospel in the symbols of a different culture, we are to avoid syncretism, that is, merging the gospel with the culture, resulting in the loss of the announcement of the Good News. Jesus is the one full disclosure of God, the one Redeemer, the risen Lord who is head of the church. However, we do not simply repeat first-century propositions, we interpret Jesus in the cultural setting in which we in the church today go about our mission. As a community interpreting the Word, we do this 188 with integrity before Christ, even with the risk of limited communication in cultures we do not fully understand. In his book *No Other Name*, Vissert Hooft, former secretary of the World Council of Churches, wrote, "Our desire to arrive at a truly adequate communication of the Gospel must be stronger than our fear of syncretism."[2]

Former archbishop William Temple defined evangelism as "the winning of men to acknowledge Jesus Christ as their Savior and King, so that they may give themselves to His service in the fellowship of the Church." Such a conversion to Christ is a change of direction, a reorientation of the whole life of a person. In *The Call to Conversion*, written by Jim Wallis of Sojourners, a community of evangelicals in Washington, D. C., who are working to develop a conscience on peace, Wallis called us to recognize that acknowledging Christ as Savior involves a total reordering of one's life, its loyalties and priorities. One born of the Spirit has a new Lord, as well as a new direction, motive, ethic, and purpose. One's life is new because it is reconciled to God, and this new relation is expressed by letting God actually be God in one's life.

Evangelism as a theology of reconciliation calls all persons to be reconciled to God and to all that he is doing in the world. We are participants in the totality of God's mission. We are called into a new community that regards everyone as an object of God's special love, and treats each person as having intrinsic worth as God's creation and as a person for whom Christ died.

The "Lausanne Covenant," drawn up at the 1974 Congress on World Evangelism, states:

> We affirm that Christ sends his redeemed people into
> the world as the Father sent him, and that this
> calls for a similar deep and costly penetration of   189

the world. We need to break out of our ecclesiastical ghettos and permeate non-Christian society. In the church's mission of sacrificial service, evangelism is primary. World evangelization requires the whole church to take the whole gospel to the whole world. The church is at the very center of God's cosmic purpose, and is his appointed means of spreading the gospel. But a church which preaches the cross must itself be marked by the cross.[3]

A few years ago, George Glover, church-statesman of England, said, "The early Church grew because it out-thought, out-lived, and out-died everybody around." We as Christ's disciples today are also called to out-think and to out-live our age. The church should be involved at the frontiers of thought and life. Too often we are copies of life around us, rather than a people of God. No wonder the atheist Friedrich Nietzsche said, "You Christians are going to have to act more saved if I'm to believe in your Savior." This calls for a total commitment to Christ in discipleship, to a life-style of genuine love, true justice, and God's peace.

Evangelism calls persons to Jesus Christ, and through him to the new order that God is creating. As disciples of Christ, we constitute a new community, which is to model the will of God in society. Radical Christianity is not a revolutionary confrontation with the structures of this world, but is a new community within the world's community, a "structure" of faith within the structures of society and one that interacts with the "principalities and powers." As said before, Jesus spoiled (unmasked) the principalities and powers so that we would not give our ultimate loyalty to them (see Col. 2:15). Therefore, the community of Jesus is to model in society what it 190   means to give ultimate loyalty to Christ.

A truly Christian community is wholistic. Even so, this wholism is not to be thought of only as psychological wholeness for individuals, but also as part of a community where the life-style as a whole expresses a Christian world view and order. For example, the Moravians, through the influence of Nikolaus von Zinzendorf, rediscovered mission work as the central task of the church of Christ, and they began to minister to the black slaves of the Virgin Islands and Surinam, communities of persons quite unlike themselves. The Moravians' sense of world mission expressed a particular world view.

Evangelism calls us to express conviction without dogmatism. Evangelism witnesses to the truth of Christ, but it is not a bigotry that slaps another in the face with its opinions. Viewed wholistically, evangelism shares with all people alike in God's grace. As followers of Christ, we are to care equally about the elite and the illiterate, for the sophisticated and for the less refined, for the rich and the poor. As Jim Wallis has written, "To live in radical obedience to Jesus Christ means to be identified with the poor and oppressed. If that is not clear in the New Testament, then nothing is."[4]

But we should also be aware of the tragic condition of those whose poverty is a poverty of the soul, mind, and spirit, having no sense of meaning in life. We must not permit materialistic categories to keep us from serving the poor, but we should also minister to the wealthy who are in spiritual poverty. When such persons are brought to faith in Christ, as John Perkins of Voice of Calvary affirms, they will discover the dignity that God has given to all people and will begin relating to the needy in the Spirit of Jesus.[5] This is also clear in I John, where our call as believers to love the needy in 191 deed and in truth is based on God's love, in that he laid down his life for us (I John 3:16-18).

Evangelism and social action must not be separated. Either one alone is incomplete and inadequate. Jesus modeled this balance in his ministry, personifying compassion as well as vocalizing it. He gave himself in an expression of the active nature of love. He also taught that we are to love God and to love others.

Love does not violate another personality; it does not manipulate persons. Love treats another as one would want to be treated oneself. Nowhere is this quality of love more crucial than in evangelism. To make the gospel attractive, we must avoid every encumbrance of method that diminishes the appeal of the message of Christ. The evangelist Billy Graham has, over a thirty-five-year period, modeled with increased sensitivity a spirit of respect and openness to the variety of people to whom he ministers. His effectiveness is a witness to his commitment to the Spirit of Jesus. I heard him say at Lausanne in 1974 that in the past he had related his ministry too closely to a political party, and that he would not make this mistake again. He received a standing ovation from the approximately five thousand persons who were present, a high percentage of whom were from Third World countries.

The "Lausanne Covenant," cited earlier, further states:

> We affirm that God is both the Creator and the Judge of all men. We, therefore, should share his concern for justice and reconciliation throughout human society and for the liberation of men from every kind of oppression. Because mankind is made in the image of God, every person, regardless of race, religion, color, culture, class, sex or age, has an

> intrinsic dignity because of which he should be
> respected and served, not exploited . . . . The message
> of salvation implies also a message of judgment upon
> every form of alienation, oppression and discrimina-
> tion, and we should not be afraid to denounce evil and
> injustice wherever they exist.

Evangelism is not truly biblical unless it makes clear that neither mammon, nor Caesar, is to be worshiped. The programs in which evangelists share must be designed not for their advantage, but for the integrity of communication with people. As the poet T. S. Eliot warned us in the play *Murder in the Cathedral,* "Those who serve the greater cause [have the greater danger of making] the cause serve them."

One will handle the gospel with reverence when fully aware of standing personally under the gospel. The gospel is not our truth, it is the truth of Jesus. Every hearer is to be called on to examine "the truth that is in Jesus" (Eph. 4:21), for each one is called to answer to Christ, not to the evangelist. As evangelists, we are free from bigotry when we witness to the "happening" that is also changing us. German preacher-theologian Helmut Thielicke writes, "The witness not only confesses and declares his message, he also confesses and declares his encounter with the message."[6]

Conviction is not to be confused with opinion. We have been laid hold of by Christ. We have met him, the ultimate reality. As we witness to this relationship, we become what Orlando Costas, Dean at Andover Newton Theological Seminary, calls "sacraments of God's kingdom."[7] We are a Good News people, a sacramental sign that God is at work in the world. This stands in contrast to an arrogant triumphalism, and to a dogmatism that answers every   193 question. We live with some ambivalence, some ambiguity, but we do so in faith. With the apostle Paul, even without having answers to everything, we can affirm, "I know whom I have believed, and am convinced that he is able to guard what I have entrusted to him for that day" (II Tim. 1:12).

Our society has become so impressed with the success syndrome that it belittles faithfulness. Max Warren, in his book *I Believe in the Great Commission,* tells of a nineteenth-century missionary in a Muslim land who said, "I am not reaping the harvest; I scarcely claim to be sowing the seed; I am hardly plowing the soil; but I am gathering out the stones. That too is missionary work."[8] True conviction provides a security that enables us to open the way to faith in persons rather than to try to coerce it out of them.

Evangelism calls for us to express compassion without condescension. Veteran missionary Donald Jacobs, in his book, *Pilgrimage in Mission,* tells of mission work in Tanzania, where persons with western conditioning answered questions the Tanzanians were not asking.[9] Our convictions of the truth of Jesus should enable us to hear others without being defensive about our position. We are primarily witnesses telling of our firsthand experiences.

Going into Washington, D.C., as a pastor, I have emphasized commitment to the third way, neither rightist nor leftist secularism, but the third way of the kingdom of Christ. This permits us as Christians to be selective about identifying with elements in either leftist or rightist thought patterns that are consistent with the kingdom rule of Christ. Put another way, it means that we cannot be boxed in by one side or the other. For example, politically I identify in my convictions against abortion with those who are more right

194

wing, and identify in my convictions against nuclear arms with those who are more left wing.

We as believers need the flexibility of Paul, when he said, "I have become all things to all men so that by all possible means I might save some" (I Cor. 9:22). This flexibility enables us to sit where others sit (see Ezek. 3:15), to understand people of other cultures, and to present the gospel so that they can understand, not altering the content of the gospel. We are called to avoid a syncretism that confuses the gospel with other religions, especially the syncretisms of our own society, with civil religion on one hand and secularism on the other. Although the gospel is both personal and social, in either aspect of its meaning we must be diligent to present the full gospel, never a truncated version of it.

It is caring with a love that identifies with others for their good, no matter what the cost to us personally, that engages us in a relationship of compassion. Love does not speak down to the needy. Love does not stand aloof and offer aid condescendingly. Love identifies with the person being loved. As in the Incarnation of our Lord, when he identified with us in becoming the Son of Man, so we also are to participate with others in the healing process.

The story of the good Samaritan (Luke 10:29-37) is a classic illustration of compassion. The Samaritan came to the needy man with wine, oil, a donkey, and money. He ministered with the wine for energy, the oil for healing, the donkey for transportation, and the money for the man's care. And significantly it was a Samaritan who administered these benefits. The priest and the Levite had both passed by the injured man, for they were selective in their love.

Evangelism seeks the restoration and fulfillment of persons. This calls for sincerely   195

affirming their worth (see John 4:9). Condescension alienates; it estranges persons. The remarkable prison ministry of Chuck Colson is a success in large part because he identifies with the prisoners in understanding love, in a compassion that feels with them, and in a spirit that affirms their worth beyond their mistakes. My friend Bill Leslie has succeeded in relating the gospel to ghetto problems in an inner city church in Chicago because he is authentic in his love. He has a depth of caring that identifies with the inner city people in their various situations. Gustave Perajon, medical doctor and Baptist minister of Managua, Nicaragua, has been specially blessed by God in his witness. He is able to identify with his people there, presenting Christ without being dominated by competing ideologies.

Again, the "Lausanne Covenant" states:

> Missionaries should flow ever more freely from and to all six continents in a spirit of humble service. The goal should be, by all available means, and at the earliest possible time, that every person will have the opportunity to hear, understand, and receive the good news. We cannot hope to attain this goal without sacrifice. All of us are shocked by the poverty of millions and disturbed by the injustices which cause it. Those of us who live in affluent circumstances accept our duty to develop a simple life-style in order to contribute more generously to both relief and evangelism.

Genuine compassion gives to another human being a sense of worth, for at its heart, compassion is taking the other person with utmost seriousness. In saying that we care, we are saying that the other person is important. After Jesus healed the Gerasene demon-possessed man, he sent him back to his friends a new man, one who carried the message of God's peace.

This was the same message that Jesus himself was carrying (see Luke 8:38-39).

To share the Good News with another is to serve that person in the spirit of Christ. In Luke 4, it is recorded that Jesus read a chosen passage from Isaiah to the synagogue congregation, in which passage he proclaimed that "good news to the poor" was directly related to ministry to the oppressed. We serve our neighbors by deeds of love, by words of encouragement, and by compassionate sharing. Lewis Smedes, in his book on I Corinthians 13, entitled *Love Within Limits*, writes that "love is personal power used to help" another.[10] Interrelating communication and service means that we identify with another in a manner that seeks that person's well-being. And seeking one's well-being has as its focus that person's reconciliation with God. Such a relationship is evangelism.

A few years ago, while speaking in Tanzania, I picked up an article written by Bernard Joinett, a French Catholic missionary, entitled "A Stranger in My Father's House." Among other things that spoke to me in this article was his emphasis on service. Joinett says that we have not truly served people until we serve them in the manner in which they need to be served, and not in the way in which we want to serve them. So long as we serve others in the way we want to serve, we are still in charge, still the "boss" figure, and have not taken the servant's stance. Hence, even our manner of service is a form of communicating. We are to model the way of peace. We must recognize, however, that service can be otherwise; it can be condescending, just as proclamation can be condescending.

It was in identifying with Zacchaeus that Jesus was able to reach him with the reality of   197 grace and the call of discipleship (Luke 19:1-10). There is no hiding that Zacchaeus was a sinner, but because Jesus identified with him, he was led to faith. The same lesson is taught in John 4, where Jesus confronted the Samaritan woman. In turn, through her witness, her village came to hear Jesus, and many believed in him.

Evangelism is, of course, witnessing with the intent to persuade. It does call for conviction and clarity, but it is not persuading persons to adopt our position, it is persuading them to accept God's position by standing beside them under Christ. We are presenting Christ, and in so doing, we are attempting to express honestly what it means for us to answer to him. Whereas our theology is the exercise of clear thinking about Christ, evangelism is basically telling people about Jesus the Christ.

Evangelism calls for us to communicate without manipulating. Evangelism is proclamation. It is a joyous announcement of the *kerygma.* It is the specific presentation of Jesus as Savior and Lord. This is the central role of the evangelistic mission, to proclaim the gospel. Some would say that for the Christian, everything is evangelism. That would be akin to an educator saying that everything is education. This can only be true in a limited way, for education involves a specific pattern of pedagogy. So it is with evangelism; it involves a specific proclamation.

We announce the Good News of salvation in Christ. We call on people to repent and believe in Jesus, to change the direction of their lives by making the choice to identify with Jesus. We help persons to pray and to appropriate the new life in Christ. We affirm them as they open their lives to the infilling of the Spirit. We incorporate them into the community of the reconciled. We seek to enhance their discipleship. We share together in the joys of worship and the responsibility of interpreting the ethical choices in life. We become prophetic in explaining the faith to a different culture, and thereby call society to recognize the will of God.

Such communicating should be done in the spirit of Jesus, by attracting people to him through honest and respectful approaches. Gimmicks that elicit a response without an authentic decision compromise the person and pervert the understanding of the gospel. And one who has been manipulated becomes further estranged from the call of Christ. We must remember that it is Jesus whom we are presenting, and we must present him in a way befitting his person. Jesus said, "But I, when I am lifted up from the earth, will draw all men to myself" (John 12:32). He was referring primarily to the cross, but the effect of his self-giving love continues. He does the drawing; it is for us as his followers to lift him up.

In Acts 17, Paul skillfully met the philosophically minded audience at Mars Hill on their own ground. Carefully and clearly he moved to the message of the Resurrection of Christ, confronting them with the claims of faith (Acts 17:22-34). Some doubted, but some believed, and Paul's strategy of presenting the truth without manipulating was used by the Holy Spirit.

The true measure of success in evangelism is faithfulness. Our tendency to measure success by "bigness" creates a false picture for us in our work. We often look at numbers rather than persons, though granting that persons comprise the numbers. Lyle Schaller's statistics, compiled while he was doing research for the Lutheran Church, tell us that 50 percent of the churches in America have 25   199 to 70 persons in attendance. The next 30 percent have 75 to 100 persons, and the next 15 percent have 200 to 350 persons in attendance. Only 5 percent of the churches in the United States have 350 to 2000 or more persons present. A proper view of the worth of persons will commend the pastors of the small congregations for their service, rather than just praise the pastors of the larger congregations for their success.

I came from a small rural church in western Ohio. From the time I was called to the ministry in the spring of 1951 until ten years later, more than two dozen persons were called to the ministry from that small church of around 200 members! Evidently the pastors were doing a significant work in that smaller setting, and they were motivating their congregation for evangelism.

Whether the setting is large or small, whether proclamation happens in mass evangelism or in a one-on-one setting, the full gospel of Christ is to be shared. Often the evangelist is thought of as focusing primarily on the Atonement, but the focus should be on the whole life and person of Christ. Jesus himself is the model for proclamation. He taught of the love of God, the kingdom of God, the new birth, the Spirit-filled life, the new community as characterized in the Sermon on the Mount, and of his own Saviorhood. Our communication of the gospel of Christ should include all of these aspects of it.

Our mission of love calls us to wholistic ministries. These include helping the poor, doing justice, working for peace amid social violence, developing family life, offering legal and financial counsel, opening pregnancy crisis centers, education, and ministry to persons enslaved by alcohol, drugs, and so on. Above all, we are to administer spiritual healing in the grace of Christ. As Australian Methodist evangelist

200

Allan Walker says of our society, "Something has been taking place which is far worse than the devaluation of currencies; it has been the devaluation of persons."[11]

But with all of our training and technological assets, we must remember that the power that enables us to fulfill Christ's commission is the power of his presence: "Apart from me you can do nothing" (John 15:5) and "Surely I am with you always, to the very end of the age" (Matt. 28:20). Jesus' presence, by the Spirit, is our strength; this is the transforming power of grace. He is the one who inspires us with "the greatest vision that ever dawned on human consciousness, the Kingdom of God."[12]

As a concluding note, the primacy of the rule of God should be seen as the ultimate reality in the world. It touches every part of men's lives. The yearning for economic justice, racial equality, political freedom, and peace between peoples, all have their answer in the rule of God. This was the message of Jesus (Matt. 6:33; John 3:3-5), and a common theme in the preaching of Paul (Rom. 14:17; Acts 20:25, 28:23, 31; I Thess. 2:12; Col. 1:13, and others). God's kingdom is composed of people ruled by the love of God in all relationships of their lives.

Although God's rule is best exemplified by the church since the church embodies fellowship, the church is not to be identified as the whole of the kingdom. E. Stanley Jones wrote, "The Kingdom is not related to something higher—it is the absolute order confronting all relatives with an offer of grace and demanding complete surrender and obedience."[13] It is life under the rule of God, in his love.

Richard Halverson, chaplain of the U.S. Senate, commented at a recent luncheon, "The problem with the American church is that few   201 people understand the meaning of the kingdom of Christ," of the actual rule of God. The apostle Paul's words to the Colossians focus this truth for us: "For he has rescued us from the dominion of darkness and brought us into the kingdom of the Son he loves" (Col. 1:13).

It appears to me that a major problem in the church is its tendency to separate the redemptive and the ethical aspects of reconciliation. As a consequence, many fail to see discipleship as an essential aspect of the reconciled life, which is the experience of the cross. But as we have seen, Paul held the two together in the second chapter of Ephesians. "For he himself is our peace, who has made the two one and has destroyed the barrier, the dividing wall of hostility, by abolishing in his flesh the law with its commandments and regulations. His purpose was to create in himself one new man out of the two, thus making peace" (vv. 14-15). Here the experience of the cross integrates the redemptive and the ethical. Ethics is not a works-righteousness, it is rather a discipleship in grace. Personal or social peace is not an addendum, it is an essential aspect of reconciliation.

A christological interpretation of Scripture will treat the new life as the expression of reconciliation. We can now relate ethics to Christology in the same way we relate salvation to Christology. Concerns for peace, love, and justice are not added to the faith experience, but are a part of an evangelical faith. Concern for the poor is an extension of the experience of God's love for us, just as forgiving others is directly related to our experiencing God's forgiveness. In Jesus' high priestly prayer, he said, "As you sent me into the world, I have sent them into the world" (John 17:18).

202

As Christ cared for all persons equally, so we are sent to serve those in need.

I would like to repeat the brief statement made earlier in this book summarizing my theology: If agape love were possible without the gospel, we would need no gospel; if agape love is not possible by the gospel, we have no gospel; that agape love is possible by the gospel is what Christian discipleship is all about!

I believe in justice; but I am not a preacher of a gospel of justice, but of the gospel of Christ, who calls us to justice.

I believe in love; but I am not a preacher of a gospel of love, but of the gospel of Christ, who calls us to love.

I am committed to peace; but I am not a preacher of a gospel of peace, but of the gospel of Christ, who calls us to peace.

I believe in the value of the simple life; but I am not a preacher of a gospel of the simple life, but of the gospel of Christ, who calls us to a simple life.

We must beware of the ultimate plagiarism, that of borrowing great concepts from Jesus, proclaiming those concepts to others, but not proclaiming the Christ who empowers those concepts. Christianity is fellowship with Christ, and the church is Christ's fellowship of the reconciled. Such a fellowship is evangelistic, for it makes persons aware of God and introduces them to the Savior. And such a fellowship is active in the making of peace, for Christ is our peace (Eph. 2:14). This is the community of the reconciled, the expression of the reign of the Prince of Peace, which is breaking into society.

Our Lord says, "All authority in heaven and on earth has been given to me. Therefore go and make disciples of all nations" (Matt. 28:18-19).   203

NOTES

1. Lesslie Newbigin, *The Open Secret* (Grand Rapids: Wm. B. Eerdmans Pub. Co., 1978), p. 176.
2. Vissert Hooft, *No Other Name* (New York: Harper and Brothers, 1948), p. 124.
3. "The Lausanne Covenant" (Minneapolis: World Wide Publications, 1974), p. 3.
4. Jim Wallis, *Agenda for a Biblical People* (New York: Harper and Row, Publishers, 1976), p. 94.
5. John Perkins, *With Justice for All* (Ventura, Cal.: Regal Books, 1980), p. 165.
6. Helmut Thielicke, *The Trouble with the Church* (New York: Harper and Row, Publishers, 1965), p. 50.
7. Orlando Costas, *The Integrity of Mission* (New York: Harper and Row, Publishers, 1979), p. 59.
8. Max Warren, *I Believe in the Great Commission* (Grand Rapids: Wm. B. Eerdmans Pub. Co., 1976), p. 178.
9. Donald Jacobs, *Pilgrimage in Mission* (Scottdale, Pa.: Herald Press, 1983), p. 24.
10. Lewis B. Smedes, *Love Within Limits* (Grand Rapids: Wm. B. Eerdmans Pub. Co., 1978), pp. 12-14.
11. Allan Walker, *The Whole Gospel for the Whole World* (Nashville/New York: Abingdon Press, 1957), p. 38.
12. Ibid., p. 43.
13. E. Stanley Jones, *Mastery* (Nashville/New York: Abingdon-Cokesbury Press, 1948), p. 128.

BIBLIOGRAPHY

Aukerman, Dale. *The Darkening Valley.* New York: Seabury Press, 1981.

Baelz, Peter. *Ethics and Belief.* New York: Seabury Press, 1977.

Beach, W., and R. Niebuhr. *Christian Ethics.* New York: Ronald Press, 1955.

Bennett, John C. *The Radical Imperative.* Philadelphia: Westminster Press, 1975.

Berkhof, Hendrik. *Christ and the Powers.* Scottdale, Pa.: Herald Press, 1962.

Birch, B. C., and L. L. Rasmussen. *The Predicament of the Prosperous.* Philadelphia: Westminster Press, 1978.

Bloesch, Donald G. *The Future of Evangelical Christianity.* New York: Doubleday and Co., 1983.

Bosch, David. *A Spirituality of the Road.* Scottdale, Pa.: Herald Press, 1979.

Brunner, Emil. *The Divine Imperative.* Philadelphia: Westminster Press, 1960.

Byron, William. *The Causes of World Hunger.* Ramsey, N. Y.: Paulist Press, 1982.

Costas, Orlando. *The Integrity of Mission.* New York: Harper and Row, Publishers, 1979.

Ellul, Jacques, *The Ethic of Freedom.* Grand Rapids: Wm. B. Eerdmans Pub. Co., 1976.

Fairlie, Henry. *The Seven Deadly Sins.* Washington, D.C.: New Republic Books, 1978.

Hebblethwaite, Brian. *Christian Ethics in the Modern Age.* Philadelphia: Westminster Press, 1982.

Henry, Carl F. H. *The Christian Mindset in a Secular Society.* Portland, Ore.: Multnomah Press, 1984.

————*Christian Personal Ethics*. Grand Rapids: Wm. B. Eerdmans Pub. Co., 1957.

Hershberger, Guy, ed. *The Recovery of the Anabaptist Vision*. Scottdale, Pa.: Herald Press, 1957.

Hershberger, Guy. *The Way of the Cross in Human Relations*. Scottdale, Pa.: Herald Press, 1958.

Hooft, Vissert. *No Other Name*. New York: Harper and Brothers, 1948.

Jacobs, Donald. *Pilgrimage in Mission*. Scottdale, Pa.: Herald Press, 1983.

Jones, E. Stanley. *Mastery*. Nashville/New York: Abingdon-Cokesbury Press, 1948.

Kauffman, Milo. *The Challenge of Christian Stewardship*. Scottdale, Pa.: Herald Press, 1953.

King, Martin Luther. *Stride Toward Freedom*. New York: Harper and Brothers, 1958.

Kraybill, Donald. *Facing Nuclear War*. Scottdale, Pa.: Herald Press, 1982.

————. *The Upside-Down Kingdom*. Scottdale, Pa.: Herald Press, 1978.

Kreider, Carl. *The Christian Entrepreneur*. Scottdale, Pa.: Herald Press, 1978.

Kroeker, Wally, ed. *The Marketplace*. Scottdale, Pa.: Mennonite Economic and Development Associates, Published quarterly, September 1985.

Küng, Hans. *On Being a Christian*. New York: Doubleday and Co., 1976.

"The Lausanne Covenant." Minneapolis: World Wide Publications, 1974.

Littell, Franklin. *From State Church to Pluralism*. New York: Doubleday and Co., 1962.

Mennonite Encyclopedia. Vol. 4. Scottdale, Pa.: Mennonite Publishing House, 1955.

Mennonite World Conference at Kitchener, Ontario. *The Lordship of Christ*. Scottdale, Pa.: Mennonite Publishing House, 1962.

Migliore, Daniel. *Called to Freedom.* Philadelphia: Westminster Press, 1982.

Moberly, Elizabeth R. *Homosexuality: A New Christian Ethic.* Cambridge: James Clarke & Co., 1983.

Moltmann, Jürgen. *The Church in the Power of the Spirit.* New York: Harper and Row, Publishers, 1977.

———. *The Crucified God.* New York: Harper and Row, Publishers, 1974.

Newbigin, Lesslie. *The Open Secret.* Grand Rapids: Wm. B. Eerdmans Pub. Co., 1978.

Perkins, John. *With Justice for All.* Ventura, Cal.: Regal Books, 1980.

Rauschenbush, Walter. *The Theology for the Social Gospel.* New York: Macmillan Co., 1917.

Schillebeeckx, Edward. *Jesus: An Experiment in Christology.* New York: Crossroad Pub. Co., 1981.

Scott, Waldron. *Bring Forth Justice.* Grand Rapids: Wm. B. Eerdmans Pub. Co., 1980.

Sharp, Gene. *Social Power and Political Freedom.* Boston: Porter Sargent Publishers, 1980.

Smedes, Lewis B. *Love Within Limits.* Grand Rapids: Wm. B. Eerdmans Pub. Co., 1983.

———. *Mere Morality.* Grand Rapids: Wm. B. Eerdmans Pub. Co., 1983.

Snyder, Howard A. *The Community of the King.* Downers Grove, Ill.: Inter-Varsity Press, 1978.

Sparks, Allister. *The Washington Post.* 2 October 1985.

Stringfellow, William. *An Ethic for Christians and Other Aliens in a Strange Land.* Waco, Tex.: Word, 1973.

Thielicke, Helmut. *The Trouble with the Church.* New York: Harper and Row, Publishers, 1965.

Walker, Allan. *Breakthrough: The Rediscovery of the Holy Spirit.* Nashville/New York: Abingdon Press, 1969.

———. *The Whole Gospel for the Whole World.* Nashville/New York: Abingdon Press, 1957.

207

Wallis, Jim. *Agenda for a Biblical People.* New York: Harper and Row, Publishers, 1976.

———. *The Call to Conversion.* New York: Harper and Row, Publishers, 1982.

———. *Waging Peace.* New York: Harper and Row, Publishers, 1982.

Warren, Max. *I Believe in the Great Commission.* Grand Rapids: Wm. B. Eerdmans Pub. Co., 1976.

Weber, Max. *The Methodology of the Social Sciences.* Glencoe, Ill.: Free Press, 1949.

Winter, Gibson. *Love and Conflict.* New York: Doubleday and Co., 1958.

Yoder, John Howard. *The Legacy of Sattler.* Scottdale, Pa.: Herald Press, 1973.

———. *The Politics of Jesus.* Grand Rapids: Wm. B. Eerdmans Pub. Co., 1972.

———. *Reinhold Niebuhr and Pacifism.* Scottdale, Pa.: Herald Press, 1963.

———. *If a Violent Person Threatened to Harm a Loved One . . . What Would You Do?* Scottdale, Pa.: Herald Press, 1983.

———. *When War Is Unjust.* Minneapolis: Augsburg Pub. House, 1985.